HOME AND SCHOOL IN MULTICULTURAL BRITAIN

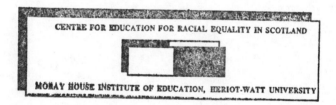

CENTRE FOR EDUCATION FOR RACIAL EQUALITY IN SCOTLAND

MORAY HOUSE INSTITUTE OF EDUCATION, HERIOT-WATT UNIVERSITY

Education in a Multicultural Society

Series Editor: Maurice Craft
Professor of Education
University of Nottingham

Titles published:
THE MULTICULTURAL CURRICULUM
James Lynch

LANGUAGE IN MULTICULTURAL CLASSROOMS
Viv Edwards

Home and School in Multicultural Britain

Sally Tomlinson

Batsford Academic and Educational Ltd
London

© Sally Tomlinson 1984
First published 1984

Typeset by Valentine Press Ltd., Rayleigh, Essex.
and printed in Great Britain by Dotesios (Printers) Ltd.
Bradford-on-Avon, Wiltshire.
for the publishers
Batsford Academic and Educational Ltd
4 Fitzhardinge Street, London W1H 0AH

British Library Cataloguing in Publication
Data

Tomlinson, Sally
    Home and school in multicultural Britain. —
    (Education in a multicultural society)
    1. Minorities — Great Britain
    I. Title   II. Series
    941.085'8   DA125.A1

ISBN 0 7134 1490 1

Contents

Acknowledgements

During the writing of this book I became acutely aware of the absence of discussion and paucity of literature about relationships between minority homes, communities and schools. There is much exhortation about what 'ought' to happen to improve and further relationships, but little actual knowledge and information. I would like to thank the following people who have read draft chapters and discussed issues concerning home and school in multicultural Britain with me: Alissandra Cummins, Maurice Craft, Janet Finch, Heather Shaw, Olwen Yates. Also thanks to Mel Chevannes and Frank Reeves for material on the Black Arrow supplementary school, Wolverhampton; to Dr. Alistair MacBeth, University of Glasgow, for allowing me to quote from draft chapters of his report, *The Child Between* (MacBeth, 1983); and thanks to Routledge and Kegan Paul for allowing me to quote at length from Nel Clark's chapter, *Datchwyng Saturday School*, in Ohri, A., Manning, B. and Curno, P. (eds.) *Community Work and Racism* (RKP, 1982).

Sally Tomlinson
Lancaster, July 1983

Editor's Preface

It is now coming to be more widely recognised that Britain is a culturally diverse society, and has been for centuries. Variations of belief and behaviour according to region, religion, class and ethnicity have always existed, but we are now increasingly conscious of the greater potential for enrichment – as well as for conflict – that these variations make possible. This new series will seek to explore some of the more salient educational issues presented by cultural diversity, and with particular reference to *ethnicity*. It will aim to contribute to the skills and understanding of teachers, teacher trainers, educational administrators and policymakers, whose concern is to provide for the educational needs of all children growing up in a multicultural society.

Home and School in Multicultural Britain considers that vital interface between the State school system and the consumer, and is the first extended treatment of relationships between teachers and minority parents yet to appear. Dr Tomlinson, a leading specialist in race relations and multicultural education, presents a systematic analysis both of present provision and of developing needs, and devotes much attention to the perceptions and aspirations of ethnic minority parents.

Maurice Craft
University of Nottingham

Introduction

Post-war migration world-wide has meant that many countries, particularly industrialised countries in need of labour in the 1950s and 1960s, have been faced with the task of incorporating ethnic minority children into education systems designed for the majority society. In Britain, in the 1980s, the education system is just beginning to come to terms with the changes necessary to assist in the creation of a stable multiracial, multicultural society, and face up to the problems involved in the successful incorporation of minority children into schools.

The successful education of minority pupils depends a great deal on co-operation, communication and mutual understanding between parents and teachers; on what are termed 'home-school relations'. Indeed, home-school and community relations have emerged as a crucial area which must be improved if minority pupils are to be offered a fair and equal education alongside their white indigenous peers. It is not, however, just relations between minority group homes and schools which are important. Schools which are changing and adapting to a multicultural society, whether in areas of ethnic minority settlement or in 'all-white' areas, will have to make special efforts to involve, inform and educate all parents. This book explores some of the issues, problems and conflicts that have emerged over the past twenty years, concerning home-school relations in a multicultural society. It starts from the premise that conflicts and misunderstandings were bound to arise. Parents who were immigrants into Britain and educated in colonial education systems, initially lacked information and knowledge about the education system their children were entering. Majority society parents, having during their own schooling been given little understanding of other races and cultures, are often hostile to the presence of minority pupils in what they still regard in many cases as 'their' schools. Little provision was made, until very recently, to equip teachers during their training with any multicultural awareness, and many teachers have lacked information to help them understand the home and cultural backgrounds of minority children, and how to teach them effectively. In addition, home-school encounters have always taken place within a society marked by racial hostility and intercultural suspicion, rather than by harmony.

There are no easy answers to problems and conflicts between homes and schools in a multicultural society. Teachers are constantly required to be agents of change in a society which seldom appears to want change. In the current state of development of a multiracial, multicultural society, many changes are being demanded of schools and teachers which they are not in a position to make. Nevertheless, this book, addressed primarily to educational practitioners, takes the view that in their day-to-day tasks of teaching and working with all parents, practitioners will find their tasks easier if they are more knowledgeable and have thought critically about why conflicts and problems arise.

In the early 1960s, a 'host-stranger' model was proposed to explain the state of British race relations (Patterson 1963). In the 1980s there are no 'hosts', we are all, majority and minority communities alike, strangers in a new multiracial, multicultural society, and we all need information and understanding on which to base our actions. Although this book makes use of the term 'minority' or 'ethnic minority' parent, it is primarily referring to non-white parents, as the continued social importance given to race and colour over and above cultural difference makes life particularly problematic for these parents.

A crisis of confidence

Minority home, school and community relations are, in the early 1980s, in a critical period. There is mounting evidence to suggest that minority parents expect a great deal from the education system, far more, in many cases, than indigenous parents. Many parents, particularly those of West Indian origin, are expressing dissatisfaction with education, and are more vocal in their criticisms of schools and teachers. The Rampton Committee of Enquiry into the education of ethnic minority pupils, reporting in 1981, regretted that a wide gulf of mistrust and misunderstanding appeared to be growing between schools and minority parents.

> The parents appear to be losing confidence in what schools are teaching their children, and schools seem to be having only limited success in explaining their aims and practices to parents.
> (Dept. of Education and Science 1981 (a), p.41).

Education is a major means whereby people from former colonial countries expect their children to join the established social order and gain access to better occupations and life-styles than they themselves enjoyed. Parents who were themselves immigrants, particularly from Caribbean countries, the Asian sub-continent, East Africa and Hong

Kong have always been eager for their children to take advantage of a system which appears to promise economic and social rewards via the acquisition of credentials and qualifications.

However, they have become increasingly anxious that schools are not equipping their children to compete with indigenous white children for jobs. These anxieties have been intensified as the economic recession and growing unemployment has meant that more qualifications are being demanded of school leavers, to compete in a shrinking job market or to go on to higher education. The issue of achievement in school has become a dominant concern for minority communities, and many parents are less willing to accept explanations that home and family factors are primarily responsible for their children's poor school progress. Some black parents have lost faith in the ability of existing schools to improve things for their children, and there have been suggestions that forms of segregated education may be the only way, in the short-term, to improve school achievement (Woodford, 1982). Other parents, while wishing their children to remain in ordinary state schools, feel that black parents should attempt to influence schools and teachers more positively. A black parent-governor recently asserted, 'We believe that black underachievement can only be analysed and corrected by blacks themselves' (Neil, 1982), and there has been a sustained growth of black supplementary schools. Minority parents are also increasingly expressing their desire that cultural diversity be genuinely respected and minority cultures taken seriously in schools. Muslim parents are increasingly in conflict with the secularised, co-educational Western education system, and have become more vocal in asserting their own community needs and values. The crisis of confidence between minority homes, communities and schools partly takes the form of a questioning of the ability of schools to educate minority pupils in accordance with principles of social and racial justice (i.e in providing equality of opportunity for all pupils), and of the willingness of schools and the education system genuinely to accept cultural differences.

The educational response
The response of schools and teachers to this crisis of confidence remains mixed. On the whole, education in Britain is pervaded by liberalism and by a professionalism which is concerned to advance the interests of all pupils. However, there is genuine bewilderment on the part of many teachers as to how to respond to minority parents and community wishes. To some extent, this is because schools are not, in any case, flexible in their response to parents, partly because a liberal stance prefers not to single out particular groups of parents for particular

treatment, and partly because lack of knowledge and poor communication may inhibit teachers from understanding minority community needs and wishes. There is also a problem in defining 'minority community' and deciding whether the views of community leaders are representative. Some teachers are retreating into defensive positions, feeling threatened by a situation they cannot understand. One head-teacher recently argued in the columns of the *Times Educational Supplement* that:

> Some teachers . . . would argue that the responsibility for the adaptations and adjustments involved in settling in a new country lies entirely with those who have come here to settle and raise families. (Honeyford, 1982).

However, there is an encouraging number of LEAs and schools who take the view that the school system also has a responsibility to adapt and change. Minority parents have done a good deal of changing and adjusting which has not yet been matched by changes in schools. Some LEAs have produced policy statements, with suggestions for improved minority home-school contacts, and a number of schools around the country are making positive attempts to contact, involve and inform minority parents.

Plan of the book
The book begins by discussing, on a general level, home-school relations and the place of parents in education as a context for understanding home-school relations with minority groups. This chapter stresses that although in Britain 'normal' home-school relations have never been particularly close or harmonious, recently more efforts have been made to inform and involve parents. The second chapter focuses on the background of ethnic minority parents, through a discussion of available research literature. This chapter notes that much of the early (1960s) literature was sometimes simplistic and encouraged stereotyping, but points out that there is now a variety of more sophisticated literature – some of it produced by minority academics – to inform teachers about the occupational, educational, linguistic, religious and cultural backgrounds of minority groups. The social class position and colonial educational backgrounds of parents, and some intergenerational problems, are also noted here. Chapter Three points to the difficulties which teachers – mainly white, middle-class and ethnocentrically educated – have in understanding minority parents and their home backgrounds, and to the paucity of research on teachers' views. Low teacher expectations of some minority pupils, poor teacher-training and the situation of ethnic minority teachers are commented on, and some suggestions for improved practice are made. Chapter Four examines the

way in which minority parents view school, and their high expectations of education. This chapter uses three research studies to illustrate parental knowledge of, opinion of, and expectations of schools and concludes that there is a mismatch between these expectations and what schools can actually offer. This mismatch may rest ultimately on the existing structures and functions of the education system and on its cultural content. Chapter Five documents some minority initiatives in education which have taken the form of additional or supplementary schooling, and describes some of the current moves towards segregated education by some West Indian, Muslim and Sikh parents. This chapter notes particularly that while religious, cultural and linguistic supplementary education provided by the Asian communities has generally been regarded as necessary to preserve and develop cultural traditions, the supplementary and segregated school initiatives supported by some West Indian parents have developed as a result of dissatisfactions with state education. Chapter Six points to the general difficulty of defining 'good' home-school relations, but uses some LEA, school and teacher initiatives to illustrate that more attempts to put 'good practices' into operation are currently being made. This chapter also discusses some problem areas, notably white parents' views of minority parents and pupils, problems of liaison and communication with minority homes, and definitions of the teachers' role in home-school relations. Chapter Seven notes the paucity of pre-school provision for ethnic minority children and raises the dilemmas inherent in introducing children to life in 'two cultures', but documents some of the good practices being attempted at pre-school level.

The final chapter reiterates that problems, conflicts and misunderstandings are bound to arise as schools, teachers and minority group parents struggle to understand each other better and work for what is, after all, a common goal – the improved education of the children. Ethnic minority parents *must* feel that their children are getting a 'fair deal' from the education system, but unless there are changes this fair deal may remain illusory. Equally, some minority parents and communities will have to face up to dilemmas inherent in providing 'equality of opportunity' for their children, while encouraging cultural diversity and respect for cultural identity. Only much more dialogue and contact between schools and parents will make it possible for problems to be solved. We should be thinking in terms of structured national policies to further relations between home and school, rather than leaving it to the initiative of a few LEAs and schools to take the lead. Repeating recommendations and exhortations is no substitute for action.

1 Home and school

Home-school relations have never figured large as a priority in British education, and we actually know very little about the purpose and effectiveness of home-school contacts. This chapter briefly examines some general aspects of home-school relations – parents and education, contact and communication between home and school, and current developments in parental participation – as a background to understanding home-school relations with minority groups.

Parents and education
Sharrock (1980) has pointed out that there is still no social history analysing the historical development of home-school relations, but much of the information available indicates that 'normal' parent-school relations have often been marked by tension and misunderstanding and, occasionally, by direct conflict. The type of compulsory education offered to pupils from 1870 onwards and the competitive, individualistic nature of the education system may have created pre-conditions for mistrust. Teachers in state elementary schools, as Grace (1978) has indicated, were engaged in a dual task of 'civilising and controlling' pupils in mass education, and many parents did not take kindly to this mission. Gautry, a London teacher in late Victorian times, was pleased that education was 'gradually forcing mothers to give up their own slothful tendencies and tolerance of dirt' (Gautry, 1937) but he also recorded that some mothers, indignant at this stigmatisation, came to school and assaulted teachers! Assaults on teachers, a particularly negative form of home-school contact, have continued to be a feature of parent-teacher interaction up to the present day. Uneasy home-school relationships have by no means been confined to Britain. Waller, in his classic study of teaching in the USA in the 1930s, wrote that, 'parents and teachers usually live in conditions of mutual mistrust and enmity' (Waller 1932). However, major efforts have been made in Britain, particularly over the past fifteen years, to improve home-school relationships, and there is currently a good deal of discussion about parental attitudes to education, and the possibilities of their increased

participation and involvement in the process of education.

The aim of increased parental involvement often appears to be one of replacing mistrustful clients by satisfied ones, uninterested parents by interested ones, and 'good' home-school relations are sometimes seen as an end in themselves. However, there is no general definition as to what exactly constitutes good home-school relations. Some schools may regard an absence of overt conflict and parental complaint as an indication of good relationships, others may seek the active support and involvement of as many parents as possible in school affairs.

Much of the literature on home and school indicates that, in any case, parental satisfaction with school, and school satisfaction with home, does depend largely on children's progress and achievement, and 'good' home-school relations may be regarded by most teachers and parents as a means to the end of improving their children's educational attainment.

The literature discussing the relationship between school achievement and home factors, though produced from a liberal concern for equality and fairness in the distribution of educational resources, has tended to place parents, particularly manual working-class parents, in an invidious position. Numerous studies have testified to the differences in achievement between social classes − lower-class children achieving less well than middle-class children − and 'compensatory' education has usually included a variety of attempts to improve home and parents. The influence of the 'good home' has been extensively documented (Douglas 1964, Musgrove 1966, Craft 1970).

The supposed linguistic deficiencies of working-class children have attained folklore status (Bernstein 1973), and much popular explanation of poor school achievement has come to stress the supposed failure of working-class families to equip their children to participate in a highly competitive school system. Much has been made of the apathetic parent who contributes to his or her child's poor school attainment by feckless choice of newspaper or lack of books in the home!

The Plowden Report (1967) has been a significant influence on teachers' views of homes for the past fifteen years. The national survey undertaken for this Report indicated that parental attitudes to and interest in their children's education were factors which strongly influenced school achievement and many teachers came to believe that their own influence was minimal when set against 'poor' home background. Less widely publicised was the Plowden comment that, 'home and school interact continuously − an improvement in school may raise the level of parental interest' (Plowden 1967, p.37). Plowden stressed that active parental interest did depend very much on the level of knowledge parents had about school and their children's progress, and in the 1960s this level appeared to be low. People tend, as the Report remarked, to accept what they know, and do not demand things they have not experienced (p.38). There is some indication that throughout the 1970s the situation did not change much. Schools do not appear to be too good at informing parents about educational processes (see Johnson and Ransom 1983). The research caricature of the low-achieving working-class child and his or her low level of parental encouragement may have had more effect on teachers than is generally acknowledged, and many staff-room conversations have centred around the theme, 'what can you expect from Johnny, just look at the family!'

However, in the USA the pessimistic view that schools cannot significantly alter the attainment of pupils from 'poor' home backgrounds is currently being challenged. Edmonds, an American researcher, has stated:

> No notion about schooling is more widely held than the belief that the family is somehow the principal determinant of whether a child will do well in school.
> (Edmonds 1979, p.21)

He believes that this notion has left teachers feeling absolved from their professional responsibility to educate *all* children effectively, and more research in America is now focusing on 'successful schooling' rather than 'ineffective homes'. In any case, the working/middle-class dichotomy appearing in much of the literature may have led schools to underestimate the ambitions of working-class parents to see their children succeed in education. Roberts's (1980) research led him to the conclusion that most working-class parents have very positive attitudes to education but lack the knowledge and information about the education system and how to manipulate it that middle-class parents may have. It was unfortunate, in many ways, that the children of ethnic minority parents were entering British schools at a time when models of working-class 'failure', disadvantage and deprivation were so popular. Many teachers still argue that all inner-city children, whether indigenous or from minority groups, are equally disadvantaged. As we shall see, this is a simplistic view, and one that many parents, particularly minority parents, disagree with.

Home-school contact

Parental attitudes, interest and knowledge about schools obviously depends a good deal on actual contact between home and school. There is an increasing amount of information available now about this and no shortage of suggestions for improving such contacts. The Plowden Report (1967) documented the kind of contacts which primary school parents were developing in the 1960s. Open days, parents' evenings, 'welcome to school' days, home visiting, school reports, were all recorded, and the Plowden Committee recommended that all schools should have a special programme for contact with homes, including pre-school contacts. The response to Plowden, according to McGeeney (1969) was 'immediate and imaginative'. Many schools sought to involve parents much more deliberately than they had hitherto done and the educational priority area action-research teams set up in the early 1970s, particularly the team in the West Riding, developed some novel forms of home-school contacts and parental 'education' (Halsey 1972, Smith 1977). Primary schools have usually been more successful than secondary schools in involving parents and both are better at involving middle-class parents than working-class parents. As an NFER study in the late 1970s concluded:

> . . . The more professional the parents' occupation, the more well-off they are, the better the area in which they live, the more likely they are to become involved in their children's schooling.
>
> (Cyster and Clift 1980, p.160)

Teachers in this particular study, however, demonstrated that they had mixed feelings about parental involvement. They wanted to defend their professional integrity from what they saw as parental 'amateurs'. Parents were by no means only interested in their children's school achievement or in teaching methods. They also wanted to know 'whether their children were happy at school and whether they ate their dinners' (Cyster and Clift 1980, p.163). This may indicate that parents do see education as more than simply examination achievement.

Secondary school parents have more diverse expectations from school and this affects the amount and type of home-school contact. At the secondary level, parental interest and expectations from school, and the extent of their involvement, may well differ if the school is an 'ex-grammar' or indeed an existing grammar school, a purpose-built comprehensive, a 'creamed' comprehensive, an urban, suburban, or rural school, a 'black-majority' school, or a community school; but there are few research studies providing information on such differential contacts. The skilled manual parents interviewed by Johnson and Ransom (1980) expected various things from their children's comprehensive secondary schooling. They expected the children to acquire knowledge and employment skills but also social and life skills, and they appreciated pastoral care and careers guidance. Most of these parents did not regard school as a central focus of family life and to a few it was an irrelevant institution that their children would eventually be 'let out of'. Neither in this nor in any other research on home-school contacts and parental involvement has the stereotype of the apathetic uninterested parent been supported. Parents who do not appear at school functions – even the ones of whom teachers say, 'the ones we really want to see never come'! – often have strong views about education.

Schools obviously vary very much in their home-school contacts. A few schools still seem to regard 'sending for parents' as a last-ditch disciplinary measure, while others, for example the comprehensive school described by Harris (1980), place a premium on communicating with and involving as many parents as possible in school processes. Communication seems to be a major problem. A Schools Council Project in the early 1970s studied contacts between schools and homes in Southampton, prior to devising better strategies for contact. They reported that parents and teachers often saw the aims of school quite differently, and that 'there was massive scope for breakdown in communication' (Lynch and Pimlott 1975). Written communications may not always assist understanding. Bastiani (1978) studied a sample of written materials sent to parents and pointed out the difficulties schools faced in trying to communicate complex educational processes to parents via letters, pamphlets and reports home. Written reports on children, traditionally the most frequent form of home-school contact, have increasingly become a focus for parental complaint and an NFER study of reports is currently in progress.

The expansion of school welfare provision and support services to homes is another aspect of home-school contact but there is little information about how the recipients of this support and help actually regard it. Johnson and Ransom (1983) reported that the parents in their study appeared to know little about the specialist services. A major rationale for the support services is that their activities actually do improve home-school relations and the educational progress of children, but the support service personnel are themselves often unsure of their particular job and find their status ambiguous or unrecognised, while professional in-fighting may occupy as much time as linking home and school. MacMillan (1980) has documented the professional problems of the Educational Welfare Officers, the 'kid-catchers' of Victorian times, who now find themselves uncomfortably placed between the educational and the social work camps, and similar problems affect other support services. Home-school liaison teachers, community education teachers, educational home visitors, teacher-social workers, cultural liaison teachers, school-based social workers, youth and community workers, all face problems of professional recognition by both school and home.

Home-school contacts, and parental views of education – particularly those of middle-class parents – may also have been influenced by the variety of pressure-groups which has developed over the past fifteen years in education. The Advisory Council for Education, with its popular publication *Where*, the Home-School Council, the Home-School Liaison Association, and the National Confederation of Parent-Teacher Associations, are examples of such organisations.

Parental participation

The development of pressure groups and more widespread discussion of parental rights and responsibilities is part of a general trend towards more accountability in education. Schools and teachers are now expected to be more accountable, and more open to public scrutiny than at any time in the past. Central government is committed to giving state school parents more 'say' in their children's education, although this commitment may be rather more at the level of rhetoric than reality. The most publicised way in which parents are to have a chance of increased participation in school decision-making processes is by representation on the management and governing bodies of schools. Up to the 1970s parents had had very little opportunity to participate in school management. A study in the late 1960s recorded that only 9 counties and 11 county boroughs (out of a possible 146 at that time) had made formal provision for parents to be represented as school managers or governors (Baron and Howell 1974). The wide publicity given to the William Tyndale School in 1976, when school managers challenged the competence of the head-teacher (Auld Report 1976), aroused public interest in the whole area of school management and parental involvement in school decision-making processes. The Taylor Committee, set up in 1975 to inquire into school management, government, and relations with parents, called its (1977) report *A New Partnership for Our Schools*, and remarked that LEAs should appoint parent-governors – at least two for a small primary school and up to six for a large secondary school. By the time this recommendation passed into law in 1980 it had been considerably modified:

> The governing body of a county or controlled school shall include at least two governors, . . . elected by parents of registered pupils at the school and who are themselves such parents at the time they are elected.
> (*Education Act 1980*, Section 2, sub-section 5)

It remains debatable how much influence governing bodies do have on school processes, and also how far teachers will welcome parent-governor contributions. A recently reported controversy at Highbury Grove School, Islington, concerned 'attempts by teachers to dislodge a Labour-nominated parent-governor, because of his campaign to speed up reforms advocated by inspection' (*The Guardian*, 20.12.82).

However, teachers may genuinely feel that parent-governors do not have sufficient knowledge to participate in school affairs; as one teacher-governor remarked of his fellow-governors, 'I mentioned pastoral care and someone said, "wasn't that to do with sheep?"!' (Bayliss 1982).

Parental representation on governing bodies and their participation in central decisions made about schools does go far beyond what many schools still think of as parental participation. In many cases this is still thought of as the rather one-sided process whereby parents attend functions organised by the school or 'participate' via PTAs or fund-raising activities. It is debatable how far the 'partnership' the Taylor Report spoke of is actually a feature of home-school relations. It is also debatable how far most parents are aware of moves towards more 'open' schooling: for example, knowing that they can now read reports on schools by H.M. Inspectors, and that examination results of schools are now published.

Much more information on home-school relations will shortly be made available with the publication of a report on school-family relationships in the countries of the European Community including Britain. This study, directed by MacBeth, took as its starting point the evidence that active partnership between parents and teachers is educationally desirable, but that there are many impediments to such partnership. 'It is easier for parents and teachers *not* to act as partners and each group, . . . often prefers to operate in isolation from the other.' (MacBeth 1983, p.2). MacBeth points out that in the past steps taken to improve the quality of home-school partnership have been based on exhortation and persuasion rather than obligation, and emphasis has been on rights rather than duties. MacBeth has made some interesting suggestions for more stress to be laid on obligatory contact between home and school, which will be further discussed in the last chapter.

Home, school and minority parents

It has already been noted in the Introduction that relationships between schools and minority homes are not particularly satisfactory at the present time, although as we have seen, this can be placed within the context that home-school relationships in general are often character-ised by misunderstandings and tensions. However there is no doubt that racial and cultural differences add an extra dimension to problems of home-school relations. Some of these problems were noted during the 1970s, which was a period of exhortation and admonition from various quarters urging improved contacts between schools and minority homes.

Townsend and Brittan, who had studied 230 multiracial schools in the early 1970s, came to the conclusion:

In general, home-school relations appear to be one of the most unsatisfactory areas of life in multiracial schools . . . more than half the schools reported difficulties in establishing personal contact with immigrant parents. (Townsend and Brittan 1972, p.82).

The DES in 1974, in its report *Educational Disadvantage and the Needs of Immigrants*, recommended that LEAs should seek to expand contact between homes and schools by all possible means, and promised urban aid grants for home-school projects in multiracial areas. The DES again declared a commitment to creating a harmonious multiracial, multicultural community in 1977, and urged schools to change now that 'the education appropriate to our Imperial past cannot meet the requirements of modern Britain' (DES 1977, p.4). The commission for Racial Equality, replying to this DES document, agreed that it was of the utmost importance that teachers and minority parents should meet and learn from each other, but stressed again the unsatisfactory nature of current contacts. The Commission thought that the onus lay on schools and LEAs to secure closer contacts with ethnic minority parents (CRE 1978, p.6).

By 1980, some research was indicating that there had been efforts to improve contacts between schools and minority homes and communities (Little and Willey 1981), but on a limited and exploratory scale. One LEA replied to Little and Willey's research questionnaire that:

Great importance is paid to home-school liaison and use made of every available resource to achieve it – i.e. local CRC and minority community leaders. The authority has supported CRC initiatives through the Manpower Services Commission to appoint approximately twenty home-school liaison officers.

Another LEA had appointed a group of cultural liaison teachers whose major brief was to make homes aware of the aims and objectives of school and report back the problems ethnic minority parents felt they had. In this study, 11% of schools said they had home-school liaison teachers; but 70% commented that minority parents were less likely than 'white British' parents to be active in PTAs. Only 22% of LEAs reported sending communications to parents in minority languages (Little and Willey 1981, p.23). Improved home-school contacts with minority parents are thus largely regarded as a matter for 'liaison' by paid professionals or by community leaders, and this may not be enough to allay the kinds of anxieties minority parents have about education, which they expressed in evidence to the Rampton Committee (1981) and the Home Affairs Committee (1980). Also, the opportunity for minority parents to participate in school decision-making as parent-governors representing their own groups was specifically *not* recommended by the Taylor Committee, who wrote that:

> The importance of ensuring representation on the governing body, of ethnic groups, in areas where there is a high concentration of minorities was stressed in evidence by the CRC and NAME . . . after careful consideration we see no need to make specific provision for the representation of particular interests . . . we are satisfied that our overall proposals will result in a significant increase in local participation in school government and ethnic minorities should thus in future receive greater opportunities for participation.
>
> (Taylor Report 1977, para 4.29).

The small number of minority parents on governing bodies by 1980 prompted the Home Affairs Committee chairman to ask what measures were being taken to improve the situation. A DES official replied that it was up to Local Authorities to 'make arrangements' for such parents to be represented (Home Affairs Committee Report 1981, p.271). However, an increasing number of minority group members are being elected as local authority councillors, and they may then be in a position to influence educational decisions in particular areas. In London, for example, by 1982, 72 councillors of West Indian or Asian origin had been elected (*New Equals*, Autumn 1982).

Summary

This chapter has briefly reviewed some home-school issues and noted that 'normal' home-school relations have never been particularly harmonious, but that over the past 15 years the importance of positive parental attitudes to, and interest in, education, has been stressed and active efforts made to inform and involve parents. Home-school relations over this period may have been affected by the popularity of models of disadvantage and the stress on working class underachievement and parental 'failure'. Home-school relations and contacts with minority parents have been regarded over this period as unsatisfactory. Improved contacts are still seen more as a matter for professional liaison than minority parental representation – for example, on school governing bodies.

Before examining minority parents' views of education in more detail, the next chapter briefly documents the background of ethnic minority parents in Britain.

2 The Background of Minority Parents

At a meeting for Sikh parents in a Northern Comprehensive school, in November 1982, a father remarked to a group of teachers, 'you should read some books about us'; another parent broke in, 'yes, but they will read books about us written ten or fifteen years ago, – things have changed for us in ten, five, even two years, – what I think now, what I am like now, was not true then.'

This comment illustrates some of the problems facing educationalists – mainly white, middle-class, and educated into an ethnocentric view of the world – who wish to inform themselves about the backgrounds and lives of ethnic minority parents in Britain. Much of the literature on minorities produced during the 1960s, though well-intentioned, can now be seen to be sometimes simplistic and paternalistic. It often took a static view of minority cultures, with customs 'brought' by minorities assumed to be unchanging, and some of it encouraged stereotyping; turbans, shalwar and creoles become 'problems' to be solved, rather than cultural attributes to be respected. Ghuman & Gallop (1981) and other writers have pointed out that there has been a tendency for educationalists to make use of stereotyped labels, the most popular being 'Asian' or 'West Indian', and they pointed to the diversity of backgrounds covered by these terms. They suggest that we must now work harder at distinguishing between minority groups who have very different cultural, religious, linguistic, educational and occupational backgrounds.

This chapter reviews some of the more recent literature available to educationalists, on the backgrounds of minority parents, pointing out that despite diverse backgrounds, most ethnic minority parents have in common an education in a colonial education system. Reading about minorities may do no more than help practitioners understand their own levels of ignorance about other cultures and nationalities, but the variety and complexity of the literature is an indication that knowledge about the background of minority parents is now being taken seriously.

Early literature
The 1960s literature concerning minority cultural backgrounds was set

within an assimilationist framework, the model being that of the school as representative of the 'host' community, inducting immigrant children into their 'new background', and explaining to teachers the strange ways of the newcomers. It is noticeable that much of this literature began by asserting that Britain had had an 'influx' of immigrants, but it should be remembered that although the composition of British society was changing during the 1960s, the 'influx' has never amounted to more than 4% of the total population of the United Kingdom. Dickenson (1982) in an article on the 'numbers game' played by some politicians, provides accurate statistical information on numbers of ethnic minority people living in Britain, the majority being British citizens. A recent paper by Brass, a demographer, has estimated, on current fertility trends, that the non-white population of the United Kingdom will be some 3·3 million by the end of the century, out of a total population of 55 million (Brass 1983).

With hindsight, it is easy to criticise the 1960s educational literature as simplistic, but it was specifically designed to help meet teachers' needs for a closer understanding of the background of 'immigrants'. The literature has also been criticised as the output of white academics and practitioners; but in fact much of the research and description of minority backgrounds, — anthropological, sociological and educational, has been produced by academics from minority groups. It is not the case that only 'white majority' academics are interpreting minority cultures. Thus, for example, Hashmi (1966) a Pakistani psychiatrist, and Hiro (1967) an Indian journalist, wrote pamphlets for the Community Relations Commission explaining the customs of Pakistani and Indian families; and Hall (1967), a black teacher who became a university professor of sociology, explored the problems of 'young coloured immigrants' in a pamphlet entitled *The New Englanders*.

Some of the 1960s literature was deliberately aimed at reducing the level of ignorance which teachers in the 1960s exhibited about their pupils. Oakley's (1968) set of readings provided rather simple information about the backgrounds of South Asians, Jamaican and Cypriot pupils. The 1960s teacher would, for example:

> . . . ruefully relate his personal discovery that Sikh boys all have the religious patronym Singh, and that the dozen or so Singhs in the school could not all be brothers.
>
> (Derrick, in Oakley 1968, p.120).

The teacher of the 1960s also apparently needed help understanding the food, clothing and toilet arrangements of 'immigrant' children, and in this area stereotyping on the basis of little or no evidence was prevalent.

An ILEA inspector's report of 1967 on immigrant children actually recorded that:

> . . . Urinating and defecating in corridors and cloakrooms, *once said to be fairly common*, now appears to be unknown or very rare.
> (ILEA 1967, p.10, my italics).

An exception to the assimilationist literature of the 1960s was an excellent book produced by Morrish in 1971 entitled *The Background of Immigrant Children*. Morrish wrote a lucid and unpatronising account of the background of Caribbean and South Asian children, with the aim of:

> . . . convincing the student (teacher) that in order to understand the problems of the immigrant child, he must have more than a smattering of knowledge of the odd marriage custom, exotic food and national dress. We must regard these things as external trappings of something more vital and basic if we are to tackle the fundamental problems of colour, culture and race difference.
> (Morrish 1971, intro).

Morrish, perhaps ten years ahead of the times, made a strong plea for a recognition of cultural diversity which would form the basis for a total programme of education for a new and more tolerant type of society.

The 1960s educational literature recording the background of ethnic minorities tended not to probe fundamental questions about the social and political meanings of colour and race, and the consequences of former colonial domination, which manifested themselves, amongst other things, in relations between schools and minority homes. The impression given to teachers that minority parents were 'just like' white working-class parents apart from colour and strange customs, was often simplistic and unhelpful.

1970s literature – Caribbean backgrounds

During the 1970s assimilationist models gave way to a recognition of cultural diversity, and some acceptance of the notion that Britain was now a multiracial, multicultural society. A good deal of literature was produced during this period describing the backgrounds of racial and cultural minorities and their continuing adjustment to an often hostile majority society. Literature on Caribbean backgrounds includes studies of reasons for migration from the Caribbean, and examination of the demographic settlement of West Indians in Britain which has resulted in some urban schools becoming 'black majority' schools. (Peach et al. 1981). Lashley, himself a migrant from Trinidad, has provided a useful chapter in Lynch's (1981) book on the multiracial school, pointing out that the term 'West Indian' encompasses a thousand miles of separate Caribbean islands, and that a 'West Indian child' is something of a mythical person. There are a variety of localised studies of black settlement, for example Lawrence's (1974) study of West Indians in Nottingham, Foner's (1979) study of Jamaican migrants in London, Pryce's (1979) study of young blacks and their parents in Bristol, and Pearson's (1981) study of West Indian settlement and associations in 'Easton'. Research studies have also provided some information on the class background and educational levels of Caribbean migrants, as well as studying the extent of racial discrimination and disadvantage that West Indian migrants have had to come to terms with in Britain (Smith 1977, Rex and Tomlinson 1979).

Some studies describing the family characteristics of Caribbean parents, particularly those concerned with child-rearing, have stressed negative aspects and claimed that child-rearing patterns in some West Indian homes are detrimental to children's later school performance. These studies may have contributed to a continued stereotyping of West Indian families as somehow more disorganised and 'less responsible' than other parents. It is relatively commonplace to hear West Indian family life compared unfavourably to 'Asian' family life in Britain, on the basis of little or no evidence. The number of West Indian mothers who work outside the home and use child-minders, has also been singled out as a problem and connections made between this and poorer school performance (Rutter 1974); and the 'behavioural deviance' of black children has been put down to 'stresses which tend to disorganise family life and depress the possibilities of adequate child-rearing'. (Bagley 1976, p.236).

West Indian family forms have indeed been the focus of heated debates amongst anthropologists for the past twenty years, and family patterns in the Caribbean — particularly the stable common-law union, are different from those in Britain. However, this by no means indicates that West Indian parents, either in the Caribbean or in Britain, are any less caring or less committed to their children's welfare and educational progress than any other parents. Indeed, Cross (1978) has pointed out that failure to understand black family ties and responsibilities has imposed additional stress on black families — for example immigration control has prevented so-called 'illegitimate' children joining natural parents.

The position of West Indian working mothers has also been ill-understood. West Indian women have a long history of migration in search of work, and 'the fact that a woman can be motivated to migrate in order to achieve her own social and economic goals is never given credence'. (Phizaklea 1982, p.100). Many women migrated to Britain hoping to become financially independent, but have been disappointed to find their opportunities limited in the labour market. Annie

Phizaklea's study of Jamaican women in Harlesden found that the women's acceptance of the responsibilities for child care often reduced their job opportunities still further:

> I worked in a factory for seven years, but when my little boy started school it was difficult . . . because I had to start at 7.30a.m.
>
> (Jamaican woman in Phizaklea p.107).

A number of writers have argued that racial hostility and discrimination has affected Caribbean settlers in Britain in different, and perhaps more acute ways than Asian settlers. Many first generation settlers from the Caribbean had been educated into a system which inculcated an uncritical respect for the 'British way of life', and found it a shocking and unpleasant experience to realise the extent of racial hostility and stereotyped beliefs about black people exhibited by ordinary people in Britain.

A recent book edited by Husbands (1982) included some personal reminiscences of black migrants to Britain. One young man, who immigrated with his family in the early 1960s to London and then Leeds, recorded that:

> Ever since I can remember . . . from being very small I was always aware of being dark – black – and for a 6-year old kid it wasn't very pleasant being called 'darkie' and 'monkey', if you're dark you're considered stupid – a fool.
>
> (Husbands 1982, p.175).

In their dealings with Caribbean parents, teachers have seldom understood or acknowledged the courage and dignity which the parents have displayed over the past twenty-five years in the face of racial antagonisms. It is important now that all teachers understand the experiences black parents have undergone in Britain, and the climate in which their children have grown up.

In many black-majority schools, the alienation of some black pupils and their defensive counter-cultures, for example the development of Rastafarianism in Britain (see Cashmore 1979), are often a source of threat and despair to well-intentioned teachers. Background reading about the black experience in Britain may help teachers understand the defensive reactions of some parents and pupils. Pryce, a black sociologist, studying Jamaican settlers in Britain in the 1970s, aptly entitled his study *Endless Pressure*. His study chronicled the ways of life which young blacks in the city developed, as their parents came to terms with moving from 'slave-labour positions in a colonial society to low-paid work in the British economy'. Pryce was not optimistic about the position of Caribbean settlers in Britain. Black parents, he pointed out, has been 'toiling as citizens and workers for 25 years', but had little to show for this in terms of economic or social advancement.

Pryce's study makes more understandable the fact that the pleasant city of Bristol was the scene of the first 'race-riots' of the 1980s. But the Avon branch of the National Union of Teachers had also noted the social pressures on Caribbean parents and their children, and the slowness of social institutions, including education, to alleviate these pressures which contributed and still contribute to the alienation of many young black pupils and the anxieties of their parents (Avon NUT 1980).

Generalisations that the older generation of Caribbean migrants were 'quiescent' and prepared to do low-paid work willingly, have however to be carefully examined. Allen (1983) has pointed out that to play down the experiences of the older generation in order to sharpen comparisons with a more rebellious younger generation may not be altogether appropriate. There were undoubtedly many Caribbean parents who were prepared to accept low-paid work and poor conditions, on the assumption that their children would do better – and this assumption may be crucial in understanding Caribbean parental attitudes to education; but there are also other parents who have much sympathy for the position of the younger generation in Britain or who have grown more cynical. As one Handsworth parent told Rex and Tomlinson in their (1979) study:

> I thought the streets over here were paved with gold, but when I got here it was a factory for me and Little Black Sambo for my son at school.

The way in which Caribbean parents have accommodated to British society is complex. Their cultural history is that of an originally African culture which was partially destroyed by slavery, and on arrival in Britain they were offered an inferior position within a class-stratified British culture. In home-school contacts, teachers should now try to be much more aware of this background, even though much current literature still attempts to equate the position of Caribbean parents with that of the 'disadvantaged' white working-class in Britain.

1970s literature, South Asian backgrounds

For anyone wishing to understand the backgrounds of Indian, Pakistani, Bangladeshi, and East African Asian parents, there is now an impressive amount of literature available (see Watson 1977, Dahya 1974, Anwar 1979); but, as with Caribbean parents, it is important that the experiences of Asian settlers in Britain are understood, as well as their backgrounds of origin. There is rather more literature concerning Pakistani and Sikh Indian migrants than other Asian backgrounds, but it does now take into account a wide variety of cultural, religious and educational factors. There is also some literature documenting hostility to Asian settlement in Britain – from Humphrey and Ward's (1972) book on Ugandan Asians, to developments concerned with the new Nationality Act (Dummett, 1982), and the increased activities of the National Front against Asians (Walker 1977). It is, for example, important for teachers to realise that in 1982 the ILEA was considering building a separate school for Bengali children in the East End of London, to help prevent racial attacks on pupils.

Rex and Moore (1967) have documented the housing discrimination faced by Pakistani immigrants to Birmingham in the 1960s, and discrimination in employment and the hostility of some white workers to Asians has been noted (Smith 1977). There have also been several cases where Asian teachers have alleged discrimination in employment or promotion because of their ethnic origin (Lister 1980).

Some of the most informative work on the background of Pakistani parents, and their settlement in Britain, has been provided by Khan (1977, 1979). Her work particularly, gives an excellent discussion of the place of women in a Muslim society and of intergenerational problems. However, she does make the point that through the production of literature detailing minority backgrounds of origin (for example, describing village society in Mirpur), the idea of minority group settlement as a 'problem' might be reinforced. Description of overseas cultural backgrounds can easily ignore settlers' attempts to adjust to life in Britain, during which time customs and traditions are modified or take on new forms. Both Khan, writing about Pakistanis, and the Ballards (1977) writing about Sikhs, have stressed that the second generation – children of migrant parents growing up in Britain – are not necessarily living 'between two cultures' but are creating new cultural traditions, and sustaining some old ones.

The majority of Pakistani and Bangladeshi settlers in Britain are Muslims, and it has always been likely that conflicts would arise between Muslims and British society, particularly now that a world-wide resurgence of Islamic traditions is challenging Western secular values. Jeffery, who studied Pakistanis living in Bristol in the 1970s, pointed out that 'Muslims come to Britain with firm but negative views about Britain, and their criticism of British morality is an important element in the boundaries thay have erected to protect their private activities.' (Jeffery 1976, p.151).

Major points of conflict concern the education of girls, the place of women in society, and the ways in which Muslim girls are expected to behave. The issue of arranged marriages particularly has always provoked anxiety and often criticisms from teachers. Ahmed (1981), herself a social worker, has noted that the 'plight' of Asian girls growing up in a socially permissive British society, while being expected to conform to family traditions, has always attracted a good deal of media attention. However, Brah (1978) who interviewed young Asian boys and girls in West London, reported that in her research, 'the majority of my teenage informants favour the idea of arranged marriage or one of its variants'. It is likely that, despite the stress involved, young Asians will attempt to develop a way of life in Britain that is satisfactory to them, and they are by no means 'victims' of an older generation who are impervious to change.

The backgrounds of Sikhs and their settlement in Britain have been extensively studied by, for example, the Ballards in Leeds (1977), Helwig in Gravesend (1979), and Ghuman in Cardiff (1980). This work has also been concerned with the adjustment of the younger generation as well as with parental views. Despite the media 'sensationalising the casualties who run away from home' (Ballard 1979, p.109), the majority of young Sikhs, who have developed strong cultural and family ties by their late 'teens, do largely conform to family and community norms, and have strong ties with family and kin, often in the country of origin as well as in Britain. There is much in British life that young Sikhs regard unfavourably – for example, the casual attitudes to family and to education displayed by some young Britons. A young Sikh apprentice told Catherine Ballard:

> Sometimes I'm really shocked at the way English families behave. I was in a pub one night, and this lad came up to his father – 'buy us a pint son' . . . his Dad said, and he said 'not bloody likely, buy it yourself'. I was staggered, can you imagine that happening in a Punjabi household?
>
> (Ballard 1979, p.115)

On the other hand, implicit in this story is the acceptance by the Sikh lad that 'going to the pub' was now a normal occurrence for him.

The Ballards have ably demonstrated the attitudes of Sikh parents towards their children. Some parents steer a careful line between maintaining Indian family cohesion and respect and allowing their children more 'freedom', others are afraid to recognise the changes inevitable in their children's future lives. One unforeseen aspect of migration to a country where many parents had language problems, has been that some parents have come to rely on their children as interpreters and as sources of information about British society.

The background of Asian migrants forced to leave East Africa and settle in Britain between 1968 and 1972 is not well-documented, but there are obvious differences between East African Asian backgrounds and South Asian backgrounds. The former, as Humphrey and Ward (1972) have documented, became, under colonial direction, 'middle-class middle-men' in Kenya and Uganda. Marett (1976) has commented on the aspirations of 'middle-class' Ugandan Asians for their children's education.

Overall, Asian parents in Britain are seeking varieties of what Morrish (1971) called 'pluralistic integration' into the majority society, retaining aspects of their culture of origin, but accommodating to change where necessary. This is not an easy process – as a Jat Sikh respondent told Helwig, in his Gravesend study, 'we have one foot in England and one in India – and it hurts in the middle'. (Helwig 1979, p.96).

As with Caribbean parents, educationalists often assume that the major problems facing the majority of Asian settlers concern their 'disadvantaged' background, employment problems and inner city living conditions. However, recent literature indicates that the settlers actually regard their major problems as racial discrimination, harassment, and threatened repatriation. Helwig's informant, on being asked what Asians in Britain actually want, said:

> We only want two things from Britain – one, assurance that we will not be kicked out, and two, the freedom to work and move about without fear of harassment from racialists.
>
> (Helwig, p.144).

1970s literature – other backgrounds
Chinese
It was noted in the introduction that this book was particularly concerned with non-white minorities in Britain, as the continued social importance given to colour and race in Britain makes life particularly problematic for non-white parents. However, it is interesting to note that Chinese settlers in Britain, primarily from Hong Kong, have not attracted the same degree of antagonism as Caribbean and Asian settlers. Watson (1977), who has studied Chinese settlement, considers that the Chinese are the least 'assimilated' of all minority groups, but that this is largely by choice. The economic niche in which the majority of Chinese work – the restaurant trade – has allowed them to work and prosper in Britain without changing their way of life to suit British expectations.

The background of Chinese migrants to Britain, and the development of their economic, political and social institutions in Britain have been written about by Broady (1955), Ny (1968), Jones (1979), Watson (1977), and Wang (1982). Jones concluded:

> At present the Chinese are still not interested in assimilation, – many do not even bother to learn English, – they retain their ability to pass unnoticed in the wider community.
>
> (Jones 1979, p.401).

But he warned that these attitudes may change when the younger generation of Chinese children — passing through British schools — grow to maturity and attempt to move into other employment. Wang (1982), a community relations worker in Liverpool, has also commented that the Chinese are not affected by racism in the way that other former colonial immigrants may be:

> The Chinese are composed of hundreds of different ethnic groups and have spent hundreds of years working through racism.

However, he does think that there are inter-generational problems in Britain's Chinese community. Parents wish to retain their cultural traditions and are afraid of 'losing' their children to Western influences. For example, many of the children are now unable to read or write the home language — usually Cantonese.

The educational level of the majority of Chinese migrants is relatively low in terms of qualifications, and there is little research on the progress of Chinese children in British schools. Jackson and Garvie (1974) regretted what they saw as poor educational progress on the part of the children. Wang (1982) also thinks Chinese children do not, on the whole, aim for higher educational qualifications, often because parents prefer their children to join family businesses. Lack of actual knowledge about the progress of the relatively small number of Chinese children in British schools, and the desire of Chinese parents to preserve a cultural separateness, do pose problems for home-school relations which have a different base to those between schools and other minority groups.

West Africans

The background of West African families in Britain is not well-documented, and general antagonism towards 'blacks' in Britain has led to some black minority members designating themselves as Afro-Caribbean. However, there are important differences between Caribbean and West African migrants to Britain. Ellis (1978) has pointed out that 'it is the search for education that has led to the presence of substantial numbers of West Africans in Britain'. She documents the movement of West African parents to Britain to further their own educational qualifications, as there has been, throughout the century, an intense interest in education, an enthusiasm for schooling, and an appreciation of the importance of education in West African countries. Many migrant parents return on completion of their education, and Ellis and others have documented the problems consequent upon the fostering of West African children with white families, while their parents study.

Goody and Groothues (1977) in particular have attempted to show why education in England continues to be very important to ambitious West Africans, and to demonstrate why West African couples attempt to meet the conflicting demands of earning a living, studying and rearing a family, by placing young children with foster parents. While English families and other migrant groups do not see this as a solution to similar problems (women staying at home is the more usual solution), West African traditions of female independence and of sending young children to other households to acquire skills and moral values, do encourage fostering. However, little is known, via research studies, of the educational progress of West African children or of home-school contacts with West African parents.

Social class and educational levels

Overall, most parents who were immigrants from the Caribbean and the Asian sub-continent had relatively few higher level educational or professional qualifications. Census information from 1971 and a national survey by Smith (1977) showed that Indian migrants were more likely to have educational or professional qualifications than Caribbean or Pakistani migrants. West Indians tended to have levels of education and skills similar to the white working class, but have usually been employed in Britain in lower-paid, less desirable occupations and have been given few opportunities for promotion. Indian and Pakistani migrant parents tended to be more polarised, being either highly educated or uneducated. Rex and Tomlinson (1979) found that 50% of their sample of Indian parents had stayed at school beyond the minimum level, but 20% had never been to school. As one Indian father put it, 'my rural primary school was six miles away and I wasn't going to walk twelve miles a day just to get an education'.

However, even well-qualified parents have had no guarantee that they would obtain employment equal to their qualifications. Smith's (1977) survey found many Asian men working at jobs for which they were 'over-qualified'. Overseas qualifications were often not accepted; for example, the DES required teachers trained overseas to re-train in Britain, and perhaps lost an opportunity, during the 1960s, of employing more teachers from ethnic minority groups.

The 1971 census also showed that women migrants from the Caribbean had higher levels of education and more qualifications than Caribbean men, although many of the women found themselves only able to find unskilled or semi-skilled work (Phizaklea 1982). Asian women, particularly Pakistani women, had little education, and often a limited command of English and little experience of working outside the home for wages. However, the image of the domesticated non-working Asian mother is increasingly a stereotype; even in 1971 40% of Indian women worked outside the home (OPCS, 1971).

Even migrant parents with relatively high levels of education have, as Ratcliffe (1981) put it, 'tended to suffer severely constrained life-chances over and above those of the native working-class'. Many East African Asians, forced to migrate to Britain in the early 1970s, found that despite being relatively affluent 'middle class' people, they were quickly relegated to low socio-economic positions in Britain. Marett, studying parents of East African further education students in 1976, reported that 'almost all the parents had suffered a fall in status on migration – nevertheless they retained values more commonly associated in this country with the middle-class' (Marett, 1976).

A small number of migrant parents have attained 'middle-class' status in terms of occupation and income, and unsurprisingly, some research has indicated that minority pupils with middle-class parents do better at school. Bagley *et al* (1979) also found that black parents with higher levels of education and occupation were more critical of schools and more demanding on behalf of their children. However, the class position of ethnic minority parents is complex and not easily equated with the class position of white parents. It is worth emphasising that the expectations and views of education attributed to working class indigenous parents are often not necessarily shared by minority 'working class' parents.

Colonial educational backgrounds

Despite the different backgrounds from which minority parents originate, the majority of them were schooled in colonial education systems, and had their own beliefs and expectations of education shaped by their experiences in colonial schools. But colonial schools were, by and large, set up to benefit the colonisers rather than the colonised, and the school systems were often parodies or distortions of schools in the metropolitan country. Basu, in an analysis of the Indian education system, pointed out that 'education is one instrument by which colonial powers sought to maintain and strengthen their domination over dependent areas' (Basu 1978, p.53). She adds that one way in which this was done was to substitute the coloniser's language as a means of communication and education, and to denigrate 'mother tongues' as inferior.

The education system set up in the Indian sub-continent, the British West Indies, East and West Africa, and Hong Kong, in which many of the parents of minority children now in British schools were educated, were all colonial education systems, although they exhibited differences. In India, for example, a Western-style education began to be seen as a means to acquire status and social mobility as early as 1844, when government job preference was given to Indians with an 'English' education. There was a concentration on urban, elite education, and a neglect of mass primary education, and the system became top-heavy. Secondary school matriculation exams were conducted in English until 1937, and universities modelled, from 1857, on London University. Basu has written that learning in English – a foreign language – led many Indian children to 'mechanical repetition of half-understood sentences'. There was a high premium placed on memory work and examinations rather than creative thinking, and the universities of the metropolitan country were regarded as a pinnacle of achievement. Indeed, Tinker wrote in 1979 that 'a quarter of the world's population was encouraged to think that the apogee of education was found only, or mainly, at Oxford or Cambridge' (Tinker 1979). An understanding of the education system of the Asian sub-continent, and its 'distorted' development under colonialism, may help teachers understand conflicting South Asian parental attitudes to education. For example, an Indian parent from an urban area, with a higher education even though working in an unskilled job, may expect his child to do well in school; while a rural, semi-literate parent might regard the fact that his children attend school at all as a major achievement. It is certainly likely that nearly all minority parents do regard secondary and higher education as a major means to social and occupational mobility, particularly, as Goody and Groothues (1979) have noted, West African parents.

In the British West Indies there was a concentration on primary education, to produce a plantation workforce, and a neglect of secondary education. Providing secondary or higher education was not a priority for the West Indian colonial administration. Foner (1979) wrote that in the Jamaican village she studied, no child, before 1953, had ever been to a secondary school. An 11 + type of selection, and fee-paying, is still retained in some Caribbean territories, and pupils are prepared for examinations in a system dominated by a traditional English curriculum. Education in the West Indies, as in West Africa, is highly regarded, and many families work hard to finance their children's schooling. Caribbean parental views of education in Britain may well be affected by their own experiences in colonial primary schools. Lack of provision meant large classes, strict discipline and rote learning, on the model of 'Victorian' schooling. The legacy of the whip in the slave plantations may have contributed to beliefs in the efficacy of corporal punishment, and the denigration of local dialects meant that standard English speech patterns were valued more than dialects.

However, while an understanding of the legacy of colonial educational experiences is crucial for teachers hoping to understand minority parents' views of education, beliefs and expectations are not static. Parents' encounters with British schools and the experience they see their children undergoing in Britain have modified or changed their views and this will be explored further in Chapter Four.

Summary

This chapter has reviewed some of the literature on non-white minority parental backgrounds, and has pointed out that in the 1960s the literature was often simplistic and patronising, and may unwittingly have contributed to stereotyped views of minority cultural backgrounds as static and problematic. The 1970s background literature is more prolific and sophisticated, giving more understanding of the complexities of relationships between minority groups with widely different backgrounds, and an often hostile white majority society. Most minority group parents, however, share colonial educational backgrounds, and their own social class and educational experiences may well continue to influence their views about education in Britain. Before moving on to examine these views in detail, teachers' views of minority parents and pupils are discussed.

3 Teachers' Views of Parents and Pupils

They dump their kids at the school door in the first year, then they come back five years later and want to know why they aren't brain surgeons.
(Cultural liaison teacher, BBC TV Multi-Cultural Education Series, 1981).

Teachers' attitudes are our number one problem – they can't communicate with us parents.

(West Indian parent, Nottingham, 1982)

The above comments made by a teacher at a multiracial school with a good record of academic performance for all its pupils, and a West Indian youth worker parent, illustrate the gulf of misunderstanding and frustration that can exist between teachers and ethnic minority parents. The next two chapters will demonstrate that, despite many good intentions, there is a mismatch of expectations between what teachers and schools think they can offer, and what minority parents expect of education. In particular, this chapter suggests that many white teachers lack knowledge about minority parents and children, and often hold negative and inappropriate views and expectations, particularly about pupils and parents of West Indian origin. Teachers generally have no clear conception of the importance of their role in a multiethnic society, and teacher training must bear some responsibility for this situation. The chapter briefly reviews teacher training and its missing ethnic dimension, and the position of minority teachers, before noting some suggestions to improve practice, and reduce teacher-parent misunderstandings.

Teachers' views
Teachers are crucial agents in a society which is attempting to incorporate minority children successfully into schools designed for white majority children, and to offer equal opportunity to all pupils. As the Rampton Committee Report noted, 'Teachers play a key role in meeting the needs of minority children and in developing multicultural approaches to their work.' (DES 1981, p.60). However, success in this role does seem to be hampered by teachers' views and beliefs about

minority parents. Teachers in Britain are mainly white, middle-class, and themselves educated into a ethnocentric view of the world through what the DES has referred to as 'a curriculum appropriate to our Imperial past' (DES 1977). They have mostly passed through a teacher training process which made token gestures – if any – to 'multicultural education', and seldom directed them even towards the available literature on minority backgrounds and experiences noted in Chapter Two. As practitioners they have, until recently, rarely received guidance and advice on contact and communication with ethnic minority parents, and have been left to develop approaches and practices on an *ad hoc* basis. Given this situation, it was not surprising that some teachers came to hold stereotyped or negative beliefs about minorities, and some felt threatened or defensive in their contacts with minority parents.

Understanding the views of teachers requires an understanding of their situation. Teachers have always provided an easy target for critical attack, without any proper attempt to locate them historically and culturally, within the contradictions of a society which offers on the one hand a rhetoric about multiracial, multicultural harmony, but on the other a great deal of pragmatic intolerance and hostility. Teachers also have always been at the centre of a matrix of social, cultural, class and racial problems, and they have usually had a variety of conflicting demands made on them. In particular, urban teachers have been expected to be in the vanguard of creating harmonious multiracial schools with good achievement for all children, with a minimum of assistance, guidance, resources or political will to back them up.

During the 1960s and 1970s, many teachers were committed to assimilationist and integrationist views and perspectives. These perspectives, at the time, seemed right and proper. They tied in with current liberal thinking that in order to provide equal opportunities, all pupils should be treated 'the same'; they tied in with genuine attempts to compensate poor and disadvantaged children, and they tied in with professional ideas that teachers' skills should be available equally to all children.

Undoubtedly, many teachers in the 1980s are still committed to assimilationist perspectives. They find genuine difficulty in responding to calls for 'cultural pluralism', and even more difficulty in accepting a need for 'anti-racist' moves in education. It is perhaps teachers in all-white areas who are more likely to hold to this perspective, but there are still many urban teachers in multiracial schools who cannot see any need for changes. Honeyford, the London head teacher quoted in the introduction, has also written that minority parents' 'commitment to British education was implicit in their decision to become British citizens' (Honeyford, 1982), and he has argued against minority 'cultures' in school or any form of positive discrimination for minority pupils. His views were supported in the *Times Educational Supplement* by another London headteacher (Gross, 10.12.82) and, as Chapter Six will show, many white parents are also committed to this view. However, Khan (1980) has pointed out that assimilationist perspectives which include ignorance of other cultures and ways of life help to set up 'elaborate structures of myth-making' which create barriers, not only to understanding parents, but to teaching minority children successfully. She used the example of popular stereotypes of Muslim children:

> They don't want to mix — the father won't let the mother come to school — they spend hours at the mosque — the girls have to do all the domestic work

to show that such crude beliefs actually prevented contact and communication with parents.

Similarly, beliefs about Caribbean parents, particularly mothers, along the lines of 'they all go out to work, the children are child-minded, — they all believe in corporal punishment' may have prevented rather than assisted communication with Caribbean parents. Assimilation perspectives may have encouraged teachers to think in terms of non-white children as automatically being 'problems'. As a black teacher commented,

> They (the teachers) think, Oh-the child is black, or of mixed parentage — problems! So before they have even met the child they have an attitude towards him and they expect very, very little of him.
>
> (All Faiths for One Race 1982)

Teachers in Handsworth

Although a good deal of anecdote and opinion exists, there is actually very little research enquiring directly into teachers' views about minority parents. In a study in Handsworth, Birmingham in 1976-7 (reported in Rex and Tomlinson 1979, Tomlinson 1980, 1981, Ratcliffe 1981) all the schools in a large survey area were visited and the views and opinions of teachers were sought.

This was the kind of urban area that had experienced very high teacher-turnover during the 1960s and early 1970s, and even at a time when cuts and economies were beginning to be felt, headteachers thought that there was still a higher teacher turnover in multiracial schools than in others.

In the Handsworth area in 1977, some teachers supported the local branch of the National Association for Multiracial Education, and made use of the resources of the city's department for teaching English as a second language, and a few were helping to organise a Society for the Advancement of Multicultural Education in the area. In the early 1970s, some teachers had supported a local branch of Teachers against Racism, which gave evidence to the Select Committee on Race Relations and Immigration for the 1972-3 report on Education; but by the mid-1970s, this organisation was defunct. Teachers did not appear to have contact with a black parents' organisation, nor the black community organisation running holiday and Saturday schools. This latter organisation particularly, was mainly known to teachers by hearsay rather than actual contact, and some anxiety was expressed that the organisation was 'teaching black power'.

This view of black initiatives in education appeared to be held in other areas during the 1970s. Stone reported that a black Saturday school run by a West Indian Methodist Church in London was thought to be a 'centre of black power which encouraged anti-white feelings among children' (Stone, 1981, p.160). She recorded that the local Church of England vicar was apparently sent to look round the school to check on these allegations.

A major view in schools in the Handsworth area was that children of West Indian and Asian parentage were all part of a group loosely labelled 'the disadvantaged', and that a major goal in multiracial schools must be that of 'overcoming disadvantage'. Primary school heads were particularly likely to view their pupils in this light. Their definitions of 'disadvantage' stressed material disadvantages, particularly poor housing and environment, and unskilled or unemployed parents, rather than disadvantages connected with race, colour or immigration. The 'disadvantage' approach led heads to view their schools very much in a social work/pastoral context, and away from a credentialing, examination-oriented approach. As one head put it, 'we help them as individuals rather than pushing them towards qualifications they won't get'. Several primary school heads noted their own lowered 'standards and expectations' which they felt were inevitable with a multiracial intake, and although they tried to provide a relaxed, pleasant framework for learning, they did not view their schools as places where high academic achievement could be expected.

There were distinct differences in the ways heads and teachers viewed West Indian and Asian children in their schools. On the whole the Asian communities were regarded as having legitimate religious and cultural traditions which could be respected by the schools and even capitalised on in school, although some teachers expressed anxiety over the 'strain' on children who attended mosque or temple school after normal school. While Asian children, both immigrant or born in England, were viewed as likely to have language difficulties, this was regarded as a legitimate school problem and a great deal of skill and expertise was devoted to helping the children 'master idiom and concepts', 'read for enjoyment' and so on. Some aspects of Asian community life were viewed as problematic – arranged marriages and tight control of girls' behaviour were judged by western standards; but on the whole, Asian families were felt to be supportive of schools, and keen on education, and their children were viewed as likely to persevere in acquiring some kind of school or work qualifications.

By contrast, children of West Indian origin and their parents were viewed as more problematic. Pupils were considered to be 'less keen on education', 'lacked ability to concentrate', and were more likely to need remedial teaching. Although secondary heads were anxious to point to individual West Indian children taking 'O' levels or staying into the sixth, the learning problems of children of West Indian origin were thought to be more acute than those of white or Asian children. The use of dialect, particularly in the home, was thought to be a major obstacle to the children's acquiring fluent standard English.

One head commented, 'We've felt for years that West Indian pupils have a language problem. The Department for English as a second language had the wrong end of the stick concentrating on Asians'. One of the clearest points to emerge from the Handsworth study was the different views that teachers held about West Indian and Asian parents and pupils. It was perhaps not surprising that these views in practice worked out to the academic detriment of West Indian pupils (see Green 1982 in the next section). West Indian parents and pupils were viewed overall in a more negative manner than Asian parents. The behaviour of pupils of West Indian origin was also viewed as a serious problem by some heads and teachers. At primary level, the children were thought to be more 'boisterous, disruptive and aggressive' than Asian or white children, and by the secondary level, the defiance and hostility of some pupils was seriously felt to disrupt normal school processes. One head said, 'They can get very violent, and show an attitude of "none of you whites are going to tell me what to do."' This same head recalled that when he asked a West Indian father to school to discuss his son's behaviour, the son turned on the father and accused him of being an 'uncle Tom crawling to the whites'.

Other heads and teachers noted that children of West Indian origin were trying to discover and develop a cultural identity, and quoted the local varieties of Rastafarianism and the deliberate use of dialect as moves in that direction. Most were sympathetic to the idea and felt that it was an understandable response to rejection by white society, but they sometimes felt threatened by manifestations of this cultural identity. The wearing of Rastafarian hats, locks and colours often provided an area for dissent in schools.

Teachers in Handsworth, at this time, did have differing views about the cultures and potentialities of West Indian and Asian pupils which could have worked to the detriment of the West Indians. The Rampton Committee wrote in 1981 that to alleviate this kind of situation, 'it is important for teachers to learn to know and trust West Indian parents and appreciate that they can be a valuable source of information on West Indian culture' (DES 1981, p.41). The Handsworth teachers paid lip-service to the idea that minority pupils were disadvantaged in the same way that many white pupils in the area were; yet they could specify and discuss actual racial disadvantage, particularly the racial discrimination in employment that minority pupils might face. Most teachers, in parallel with most parents interviewed, did hope that multiracial schools would provide a caring, controlled environment for learning, for all pupils, but the teachers did not have sufficient contact and communication with parents to make it clear that they shared this objective.

Teacher expectations

It was noted in Chapter One that in general, parents' views of school and teachers' views of parents are affected by the academic achievement of the pupils. Teachers' views of minority parents are particularly likely to be influenced by whether achievement is high or low. But pupils' achievement is itself strongly linked to teacher expectations. There is research, particularly from the USA, to suggest that teachers do have lower expectations of some minority pupils, that they teach according to these expectations, and that this teaching does affect performance. Teachers may then be in the ironic situation of having to discuss with parents the low achievement of their children, which the teachers themselves may have helped to create. It is not surprising that discussing pupils' performance with minority parents is an area fraught with tension. A major problem with research which links teacher views and expectations with poorer minority academic performance is that the links are difficult to show empirically, and it is also difficult to separate expectations based on socio-economic factors, from those based on 'racial' factors. Teachers often do view lower class children as being less academically able. Interestingly Rist (1970) working in an urban, black, school in the USA, found that even middle-class black teachers were likely to have lower expectations of working-class black children.

It was Rubovits and Maehr, (1973), two American researchers, who built on the well-known work of Rosenthal and Jacobson (1968) to suggest that white teachers have lower expectations of black pupils, even those of high ability. The teachers in their study did treat black pupils less positively, ignored them more in class, praised them less but criticised them more. Teachers who were rated as 'dogmatic' exhibited the most negative patterns in teaching black pupils. In Britain, Coard's (1972) influential polemical booklet on the 'ESN issue' specifically used Rosenthal and Jacobson's work to contend that teacher attitudes towards, and expectations of, West Indian children, caused them to underestimate the children's ability. He quoted teachers who were reluctant to press West Indian children academically, because 'they weren't up to it – poor chaps'. Coard suggested that the children built up resentment and emotional blocks as a result of such treatment. A decade later the Rampton Committee reported that they had spoken to teachers who exhibited 'negative and patronising attitudes' to West Indian pupils (DES 1981, p.13), and suggested that such attitudes could affect performance.

Green's (1982) research appears to be the only work, to date, in Britain, which approximates to the Rubovits and Maehr study. Green studied the 70 white teachers of 940 white, 449 Asian and 425 West Indian pupils, and demonstrated that teachers' racial (or 'ethnocentric' as he described them) attitudes affect not only expectations about pupils but also actual classroom teaching. Teachers who were 'highly intolerant' spent more time with white boys, and then with Asian boys; Asian girls and West Indian boys got least teacher time. Highly tolerant teachers give more time equally to boys and girls and more to West Indian boys. Green's study demonstrates powerfully that, on the whole, white and Asian children benefit substantially more from teacher attention in the classroom, whatever the tolerance level of the teacher, than children of West Indian origin. His research adds substantial empirical weight to previous research which had suggested logical, rather than empirical connections, between teacher attitudes to and expectations of, West Indian pupils, and their subsequent academic performance. Driver, for example, in a study of a Birmingham comprehensive school in the early 1970s, had pointed to a variety of ways in which cultural misunderstandings could arise, which resulted in teachers feeling threatened or anxious in their dealings with West Indian pupils. This could lead to the pupils being 'vulnerable to poor assessment of their abilities' (Driver 1977). Among the problems which could arise, Driver noted teachers' slowness in identifying their West Indian pupils by name, their misunderstanding of West Indian cultural gestures, and the discouragement of the use of dialect. Brittan, in a study of 850 teachers' opinions of their pupils also noted the willingness of teachers to make generalisations about pupils of West Indian origin, and to produce contradictory stereotypes: the pupils were described as lazy/passive/withdrawn, and also as boisterous/aggressive/disruptive. She wrote that 'it is clear that teachers perceive West Indian pupils as of low ability and as creating discipline problems' (Brittan 1976, p.190).

Giles, a black American professor, visited 23 London schools in the mid-1970s, and 'became convinced that there are both subtle and overt forms of discrimination taking place in British schools, resulting from teachers' attitudes and behaviour . . . towards West Indian students' (Giles 1977, p.75). One unusual type of discrimination documented by Jones (1977) and Carrington (1983) is teachers' propensity to view pupils of West Indian origin as likely to be better at sport, and to channel them into sporting rather than academic activities. Carrington has reported that some pupils actually favour sporting activity, seeing it as an opportunity to succeed, and to 'take over' an important area of schools; but many West Indian parents have complained that too much sport militates against their children acquiring academic qualifications.

There is also a good deal of evidence to suggest that teachers have, until recently, viewed the behaviour of West Indian pupils much more negatively than that of white or Asian pupils. Green (1972) recorded that teachers saw pupils of West Indian origin as being more aggressive, sulky and resentful, and creating more discipline problems. Rutter (1974) asked teachers to rate over two thousand ten-year old London children on a behavioural scale, and nearly half the West Indian boys in this study were judged by their teachers to be 'behaviourally deviant'. Tomlinson (1982) found that heads and teachers in Birmingham were more willing to stereotype West Indian pupils as aggressive, disruptive and 'less keen on work', and some teachers felt actively threatened by the behaviour of West Indian adolescents, linking this to a militant black response; one headteacher spoke of her catchment area as 'a black power area'. Mabey (1981), reporting data from the ILEA literacy survey, recorded that teachers rate West Indian pupils and their parents more negatively than other groups; they thought that West Indian parents were less likely to be interested in their childrens' schooling, and that the children did not come from 'culturally stimulating homes'.

All in all, evidence suggests that teachers hold very negative expectations about West Indian pupils concerning both their academic potential and their possible behaviour, and their views of the parents are similarly negative. Why this should be can only be a matter for speculation at the moment.

Teacher training

If teachers' views and expectations of some minority pupils and their parents are negative and stereotyped it should be remembered that they have, by and large, received little help or preparation from their training to encourage more positive views. Teachers' knowledge about and views of minorities depend a great deal on the preparation and help they receive through initial teacher training courses. Teacher training institutions have, over the past twenty years, shown little enthusiasm for preparing teachers to work in a multiracial, multicultural society, and even now may not regard such preparation as an urgent priority. There has never been a coordinated national policy to ensure that teachers received even minimal preparation for teaching in racially and culturally-mixed schools, nor to make them aware that some responsibility for putting into practice the idea that 'Britain is a multiracial, multicultural society' (DES 1977), might lie with them. Throughout the 1970s, the lack of preparation offered to intending teachers for teaching in a multiracial society was stressed in research and reports, and as Craft remarked in 1981, 'it is profoundly depressing to find the same recommendations for action appearing again and again', (Craft 1981, p.2). McNeal and Rogers, documenting actual teaching practices in multiracial schools in 1971, wrote that teachers usually came to multiracial classrooms unprepared; and Townsend and Brittan concluded that the most common feature of the 230 multiracial schools they studied in the early 1970s was the lack of adequate teacher preparation. By the late 1970s, research for the Schools Council suggested that teacher training had not improved much; Local Education Authorities still thought of teacher education for a multiracial society in terms of ESL courses (Little and Willey 1981). The DES document *Education in Schools* (1977) reported:

> The Secretary of State shares the misgivings of those who believe that too many entrants to the teaching profession have inadequate experience and understanding of the world outside education, including its multicultural and multiracial aspects.

And two major reports in 1981, from the Home Affairs Committee and the Rampton committee, expressed disquiet and irritation at the way continued exhortations and recommendations had resulted in little action. The Home Affairs Committee wrote:

> It is no longer acceptable to wait for the complex administrative structures of teacher training to come to terms in its own good time with the challenge presented by the multiracial classroom. It is against a background of justified weariness and impatience that we consider how teacher training must tardily adapt to this challenge.
>
> (Home Affairs Committee, 1981, para 138).

Several months later an HMI survey, *The New Teacher in School*, found that over half the teachers they questioned felt that their courses had given them no preparation whatsoever for teaching children of different cultural backgrounds. Indeed, they felt that the ethnocentric base of teacher training had barely shifted. As one new teacher succinctly put it:

> My training prepared me for teaching in a small, suburban primary school in a

middle class area, but not for the special priority area urban, multicultural school.

(DES, 1982, p.35).

However, there have been good reasons for the reluctance of teacher trainers to get to grips with appropriate preparation for all new teachers. For the past twenty years, there have been pressures on colleges to change and innovate in a variety of areas. Latham, himself a teacher trainer, pointed out that during the 1970s colleges were under pressure to include 'everything from Bullock to Warnock to micro-electronics to multicultural education' (Latham, 1982), and that crucial issues have often become trivialised for lack of adequate time during the teacher training period. The most many colleges and Departments of Education managed during the 1970s were optional courses for a few intending teachers in multiracial schools – although, and as a survey by Cherrington and Giles (1981) demonstrated, there were few enough even of these sorts of courses up to 1980. Eggleston, directing a· project enquiring into *in-service* teacher education, reported that in-service courses for teaching in a multicultural society were also 'fragmentary and incomplete', and that courses were often cancelled for lack of support (Eggleston, 1981). A further reason for the paucity of courses and the lack of awareness that all intending teachers might need some kind of preparation for a multiracial society, was that teacher trainers themselves were not usually recruited on the basis of their knowledge of multicultural issues, and the problem of training-the-trainers has now become crucial. Eggleston (1983) has pointed out that although there is much more awareness of the problem, colleges, denied new staff, have had to 'recycle existing staff into the new curricula, staff who do not always have great enthusiasm, let alone relevant experience'.

A further problem is that, even though teacher trainers may now be willing to innovate, they do not know how to put into practice the rhetoric of 'preparing all teachers to teach in a multiracial, multicultural society'. The CNAA, which validates many teacher training courses, has attempted to move away from the idea that a few intending teachers 'do multicultural options', and advocates that all teacher training courses be permeated with a multicultural awareness (Council for National Academic Awards, 1982). They have suggested that institutions designate at least one member of staff who will act as an agent of change, to encourage their colleagues to be less ethnocentric and more positive in their teacher preparation for a multicultural society. However, there is a risk that this could lead to one individual being associated with the multicultural element, and Eggleston (1983) has warned of the dangers of an 'ethnic naivete'. Raising consciousness and permeating courses with multicultural awareness does not necessarily foster the skills needed for successful teaching in multiracial schools, or indeed, in any schools. In the future, both curriculum permeation *and* more skills will be required.

Ethnic minority teachers

So far, this chapter has discussed the views white teachers hold about minority parents and pupils. For the past few years, however, there has been a growing lobby pressing for the recruitment, training and employment of more teachers from ethnic minority groups, on the logical grounds that such teachers could benefit minority pupils and communicate with parents in ways which white teachers are not able to.

Minority teachers, it is argued, will also provide role models for minority pupils to emulate, will help alleviate possible 'identity problems' of minority pupils and parents, and will help non-white pupils and parents see that teachers behave in particular ways because they are teachers, rather than because they are white. Gibbes (1980) who interviewed 27 black teachers in a small survey for the Caribbean Teachers Association, listed 14 special contributions which these teachers said they could make. These included:

– helping black parents, many of whom find it easier to communicate with a black teacher than a white one,

– providing a positive image for white people, helping to eradicate stereotyped views of blacks.

This last point is presumably particularly important in predominantly white schools. The black teachers interviewed by Gibbes certainly felt that the presence of black teachers in multiracial schools was essential.

There is other evidence that minority group teachers feel they have an important contribution to make to the education of non-white children, and that they are perhaps able to view the children and their parents in a more positive light than many white teachers. Chapter Five, which examines black supplementary and segregated schooling, quotes teachers at a North London black private school who felt that the staff could identify with the children 'in ways which white teachers, no matter how sympathetic, are unable to' (Woodford, 1982). The National Convention of Black Teachers, an umbrella organisation of black teachers' groups, supported a speaker at a conference who complained that 'white teachers go to Bangladesh or a Caribbean Island for a few weeks and come back as experts', when there are large numbers of experienced black teachers who would perhaps be better able to teach children from different racial and cultural backgrounds (Spencer, 1981).

However, the actual numbers of minority teachers employed in Britain are still a very small proportion of the total teaching force, and since LEAs do not collect ethnic statistics on their teachers, there is no way of counting exactly how many there are. Gibbes estimated that there were no more than 800 non-white teachers (1980), and Cohen and Manion have suggested that there may be only one West Indian teacher for every four hundred pupils of West Indian origin in schools (1983). The Select Committee on Race Relations and Immigration noted in 1973 that most minority teachers had trained abroad, and had done further training in Britain to satisfy DES requirements. The DES had set up special courses to improve the English of intending teachers, and by 1973 some 430, largely Asian, teachers had taken such courses (Select Committee 1973, p.32).

By 1975, the idea of special access courses to increase the numbers of minority teachers had been suggested. The DES had run pilot schemes, and in 1980/81, 291 students, half of whom were of West Indian origin, were attending such courses (DES 1981). They are intended as preparatory courses for students who have not acquired the qualifications to take them straight into the B.Ed. route to teacher training. The courses appear to attract women of West Indian origin, rather than West Indian men or Asians of either gender. Teaching as a profession does not seem to appeal to many Asian students who currently reach higher education in Britain. They are far more likely, as Yellim's (1983) research demonstrated, to go into medical-related professions. Rex and Tomlinson found in their (1979) study that of 305 Asian parents interviewed, none wanted their sons to be teachers.

Minority teachers, however, do seem to have specific problems in their employment and promotion. Gibbes's (1980) study suggested that black teachers had stressful experiences obtaining and keeping jobs, felt discriminated against in promotion, and consequent low morale was more likely to make them consider leaving the profession. Black teachers' groups have, particularly over the past three years, complained of discrimination in employment (Lister 1980; Spencer 1982 (a)). The Secretary of the National Convention of Black Teachers wrote in a letter to the *TES* in 1982 that:

> Although we are teachers of Afro-Caribbean/Asian origin, the problems we face in employment, jobs and promotion are not due to our ethnic origin, but because of the colour of our skin.
>
> (Ray 1982)

Also, if black teachers do move to senior levels in school it is probable that they will face more scrutiny and possibly hostitity from parents. The employment of non-white teachers in schools is probably not the simple panacea for improving black pupils' 'identity', school performance, or relations with parents, that it is sometimes thought to be.

Improved practice

Evidence to date suggests that many white teachers have, during the past twenty years, held inappropriate views about minority parents and pupils: their lack of knowledge about minorities leading to stereotyped views; their assimilationist perspectives leading to difficulty in accepting manifestations of 'cultural pluralism'; and their negative views of West Indian parents and pupils in particular, possibly affecting the academic performance of these pupils. A mismatch between teachers' views of minority parents and their expectations of pupils, and what minority parents actually expect schools and teachers to provide, does exist, and is not a good basis for improved home-school relations. However, there are indications that teachers' views about minority parents and pupils are changing. Some teachers are gradually becoming more informed, and hopefully, crude stereotyping and negative beliefs are less likely to occur. Improved teacher training does seem to be having an effect on many student-teachers, who are becoming more aware that they have some responsibility for making schools genuinely 'multiracial and multicultural'. The Rampton Report was a document actually read and discussed in schools, and there will be few teachers who have not heard about, if not actually debated, the Report. There is an influential movement in education, with some teachers working towards an acceptance of cultural diversity, towards facing the problems of accepting alternative values in schools, and of providing equal opportunities for all children; and there are teachers who are actually listening to minority parents' viewpoints. Much of this is not easy for teachers who, as this chapter noted earlier, are mainly white, middle-class, educated into an ethnocentric view of the world and harangued by demands to 'change society' with minimal guidance, support, resources, or political backing. The teaching profession is under attack from several sides at the moment, and there seems little point in attacking teachers and scape-goating them for their 'multicultural failures'. Mukherjee, a Sikh teacher-trainer, has recently labelled white teachers as 'liberal racists' who 'have abdicated their responsibility to deal with an issue that is their own creation' (Mukherjee 1983). This kind of polarisation of view may be unproductive and unhelpful, as the most promising signs of change and awareness are in fact coming from the teaching profession itself. The success of the National Association for Multi-racial Education (NAME), which has grown from a small group of teachers in the early 1970s to a relatively large and influential organisation in the 1980s, is an indication that more teachers, white and non-white, are committed to debate and discussion as to how to make Britain a just multiracial and multicultural society.[1] All London Teachers Against Racism and Fascism (ALTARF), operating in the currently Labour-controlled Inner London Education Authority, have led the debate on raising teachers' consciousness of their own 'racism'[2]; the National Union of Teachers have made a written commitment to discipline members who display 'racist' conduct,[3] and there are a few schools which have developed actual 'anti-racist' policies (see for example the school reported in *Where*, no. 182, 1982).

In addition, the Secondary School Heads Association has set up a working party to consider education in a multicultural society and is committed to dialogue with minority parents.

> We can learn from the parents and communities about their way of life, their beliefs, and their needs and desires for their children.
>
> (Review, *Secondary Heads Journal*, 1982, p.487.)

It is greatly to the credit of the teaching profession that, in an atmosphere of continued hostility to non-white members of society, most teachers are persistently, if haltingly, working in a positive direction.

However, following Banks (1981), an American researcher who has produced a model illustrating the qualities a 'multi-ethnic' teacher should have, the model below illustrates some positive characteristics which teachers in multiracial, ·multicultural Britain should perhaps display or acquire. In addition, teachers in Britain could consider following the example of the *National Council for the Accreditation of*

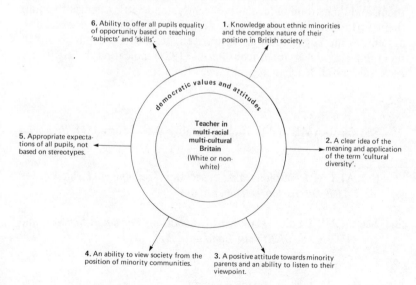

The teacher in multiracial, multicultural Britain (after Banks, 1981).

Teacher Education, in the USA, who since 1979 have made it a requirement that all teachers in America should have received some training in 'multicultural' education in their teacher education programmes.

Summary

This chapter has suggested that in the past many white teachers have lacked knowledge about minority parents and children, and have held inappropriate or stereotyped views about parents and negative expectations of their children. A study of teachers in Handsworth was used to illustrate the difficulties some teachers experienced in moving from stereotypes to genuine understanding of the cultures, lifestyles, problems and potentialities of Asian and West Indian families. Several studies, including Green's (1982) important study, were cited as evidence that teacher expectations about minority pupils did have an important effect on school performance. If, as noted in Chapter One, improved school performance is the major issue that unites parents and teachers, teachers may in fact be undermining their own efforts to improve minority home-school contact, by their inappropriate expectations of minority pupils. However, it was pointed out that teachers, who are at the centre of a matrix of social, cultural, class and racial problems, have had a variety of conflicting demands made on them, and their training has, until recently, made little attempt to equip them to function effectively in a multiracial, multicultural education system. Some suggestions for improved practice were put forward, including a model adapted from Banks (1981) indicating the attributes of a 'successful' teacher in multiracial Britain.

Notes
1. See the NAME publications, notably their journal *Multi-Racial Education*.

2. See ALTARF publications, especially *Teaching and Racism. An ALTARF Discussion Document*, 1980.

3. See the NUT policy statement *Combatting Racism in Schools*, and the NUT *Code of Ethical Conduct*, NUT.

4 Minority Parents' Views of Education

The dream of a good education for their children has always had a particular significance for black people. White colonists fed generations of Asians, Africans and West Indians the myth that the reason they were being economically exploited was not because of race or colour but because they were backward, undeveloped and uneducated. The old colonialist equation of 'education equals power' explains why so many black parents passionately wanted for their children the education they never had.

(Organisation of Asian and African Women, 1979)

If relations between schools and minority homes are to be improved, educationalists will need to understand more clearly the views and expectations that minority parents hold about education, and why those views are often held so strongly. There is to date, however, limited research evidence which might help such an understanding along. While, in general, the way most indigenous parents view education depends a good deal on their own levels of education and socio-economic background, minority parents' views are also influenced by their colonial and cultural backgrounds and the high expectations of education often nurtured in their country of origin; by their own levels of knowledge about an unfamiliar education system; and by their experience of schools and teachers in Britain. This means that minority parents' views and expectations will be different to those of indigenous parents. In particular, although most minority parents in Britain are, in crude socio-economic terms, 'working-class', their views and expectations have always approximated more to those of the 'middle-class', but without the detailed knowledge of the education system and its intricacies that middle-class parents in Britain usually possess.

Despite different colonial and cultural backgrounds and despite disappointments engendered by their encounters with the education system, both research and opinion suggest that most minority parents are anxious for their children to do well in education and to acquire skills and qualifications which will enable them to find employment or go on to further education or training.

This chapter examines the expectations and views of education that minority parents hold and discusses some of the contradictions inherent in these expectations.

Views and expectations

There is currently much scope for conflict of opinion concerning minority parents' views and expectations of schools and education. This stems from the paucity of actual research in which the parents have been asked about their views. As so often in the area of race and ethnic relations, different opinions and speculations are offered as hard evidence. In general, research suggests that whatever the class position, educational levels and colonial backgrounds of migrant parents, they mostly share high expectations about education, and they view schools as places where their children's life chances should be enhanced. Many migrant parents working in low-paid jobs have felt that their efforts might be justified if their children could acquire a more favourable position in society than *they* were able to achieve. This is not a situation specific to Britain. Rex pointed out in 1971 that an open education system may be the one means whereby occupational and status mobility is made possible for migrants in any country, and education has always been regarded by migrants from colonial countries as a way into the established social order of their 'mother' country (Rex 1971).

There has been considerable stereotyping on the part of education-alists concerning supposed differences between Caribbean and Asian parents' views of education (see Chapter Four). Asian parents are considered to be more interested in their children's education and more supportive of schools. In fact, there is little direct evidence to support this claim. What is noticeable is that more educational researchers, particularly those of Asian origin themselves (Dosanjh 1969, Bhatti 1978, Ghuman 1980 a, b) have stressed the positive interest and characteristics of Asian families; while (mainly white) researchers attempting to explain poor West Indian school performance, have often stressed supposedly negative family characteristics. Also, more research has been carried out enquiring into the career aspirations of Asian school-leavers than of other minority groups, and this research has tended to stress Asian parents' support for their children staying on in education. Foner did record, in her comparative study of Jamaicans in London and Jamaica (Foner 1979), that the Jamaican migrants to London did not accord the same status to education in London as they did in Jamaica (in London they were more concerned about racial discrimination!), but they still regarded it as very important. Rex and Tomlinson found in their Birmingham research that West Indian parents displayed an interest in education equal to that of Asian parents, and were actually rather more likely to have visited their children's schools (Rex and Tomlinson 1979).

What may be an important difference between Caribbean and Asian parents is that from the early 1960s, Caribbean parents' expectations have centred around the view that schools would be able to offer their children 'equality of opportunity' and that this would be reflected in examination passes. Anxiety and frustration has resulted from the inability of schools to satisfy these expectations. The 'under-achievement' of pupils of West Indian origin and the variety of explanations offered to account for underachievement is probably the most-documented characteristic concerning ethnic minority pupils in Britain (see Taylor 1981, Reeves and Chevannes 1981).

Asian parents, also expecting 'equal' opportunities to be offered to their children, have been more satisfied with schools, which from the early 1960s did take their children's learning problems seriously (particularly those connnected with language) and have been able to help a number of Asian children to achieve examination passes and qualifications (Tomlinson 1983). Asian parents' anxieties and frus-trations have centred more around the expectations that schools would also accommodate to cultural diversity. A West Indian father encapsulated this difference thus:

> West Indians have a different philosophy to Asians – we look on education as creditation, exam passes which we didn't have – when our kids don't pass – the world falls apart. Asians are more concerned with religion and things like that.[1]

The Redbridge parents studying the education of West Indian pupils in the Borough also pointed out that the disappointment of their expectations has been felt more acutely by West Indian parents than by other ethnic groups:

> Many West Indian adults are understandably bitter at their rejection by the 'mother' country and this may be conveyed to the youth – such parental bitterness may not be matched by other immigrant groups whose emotional links with Britain were not as deep.
>
> (Redbridge study, 1978, p.12)

This is not to say that West Indian parents are not concerned with cultural differences and an acceptance of their children as respected, black young citizens. The Redbridge parents considered that the poor school achievement of West Indian children could be traced to the effects on black children's identity of living in a hostile white society, and they wanted changes in the school curriculum and in teachers' attitudes. But, by and large, pressures to change the curriculum in a 'multicultural' direction have not come from West Indian parents. Maureen Stone, a black academic, has argued that because they are mainly concerned with achievement, West Indian parents want a traditional, basic curriculum and do not want multicultural innovation designed to enhance their children's sense of cultural identity. Although she herself has not carried out any systematic research asking parents, her views are supported in other work. Rex and Tomlinson (1979), for example, found that few of the West Indian parents they interviewed favoured the idea that 'black studies' be taught in schools, although they did support local community organisations who offered courses in Afro-Caribbean history. The debate, however, is not an 'either-or' one; the desire for equality of opportunity on the part of West Indian parents does include the wish that their children be respected, understood, and accepted in schools much more than hitherto, and this demands changes from schools in a 'multicultural' direction. Taylor, concluding her review of literature on the education of pupils of West Indian origin, wrote that the majority of West Indian parents

> . . . believe that ultimately education is the most reliable means available whereby their group as a whole, through their children, can receive recognition and status on an equal footing with others in society.
>
> (Taylor, 1981, p.143)

This can only be achieved if schools now genuinely begin to make changes in a 'multicultural' direction.

Asian parents also share expectations that their children will be offered equal opportunity to succeed, and view education as a major means of upward social mobility for them. Indeed, it is relatively commonplace to hear teachers complaining that Asian parents have 'unrealistically' high aspirations for their children. However, Vellims, in an analysis of university entrance statistics recently demonstrated that 'South Asians are proving more successful in penetrating the higher levels of the British education system than their white working-class peers'. (Vellims 1982, p.212). Aspirations on the part of Asians may be as realistic as those of any other group of parents.

High expectations were noted in one of the earliest studies of Asian parental attitudes to education in Britain (Dosanjh 1969). Dosanjh compared Sikh and Muslim Punjabi parents in Derby and Nottingham, and found that although the Nottingham parents were better educated and working in more skilled occupations than the Derby parents, both groups shared a very strong desire for upward social mobility for their children, and education was seen as the key to this. The parents did not know much about school organisation, methods, or curriculum at that time, but they did complain about 'too much play, too little homework, and lack of discipline in schools'.

There has been a variety of research studies subsequently pointing to the support and encouragement Asian parents offer to their children, particularly encouraging them to stay on for further education and training. For example, Gupta (1977) studied a sample of English and Pakistani school-leavers, and concluded that Asian parents 'did exert a clear-cut influence over their children's educational and subsequent occupational choice'. Bhatti (1978) studying young Pakistanis, supported the claim that Asian parents expect to exert much influence on their children, and he regretted the lack of home-school contacts whereby parents could make their views known to schools. Fowler *et al.* (1977) also noted Asian parental encouragement for their children to acquire school qualifications, but noted a 'readiness on the part of Asian parents to accept school definitions of what the best interests of their children were' (p.69).

Asian parental enthusiasm for school and desire to see their children acquire credentials has been matched by expectations that schools would also accommodate to different cultural traditions and arrangements in the Asian communities; and much of the continuing anxiety about schools on the part of Asian parents has derived from the persistent reluctance of schools genuinely to recognise and accept cultural diversity. Major sources of anxiety for Asian parents are mother-tongue and religious teaching, crucial aspects of cultural identity; dress and food, crucial cultural symbols; and single-sex education, P.E. and swimming for girls, crucial areas in relation to the place of women in Asian cultures. While schools serving Asian communities do not need to be told that these are important issues for the communities, research by Noor and Khalsa (1978), Ghuman (1980 b, 1981), and Tanna (1981) has confirmed that these remain central and important areas where Asian parents' expectations that schools will make changes and accommodations remain unsatisfied. Home-school conflicts and misunderstandings are therefore likely to occur.

Chinese parents, according to Wang, have never made their expectations particularly clear to schools; but like other Asian communities, their anxieties have centred more round schools' attempts to assimilate their children, rather than respect their cultural separateness. Chinese parents have not pressed for examination success, although those children who have shown exceptional ability have not lacked home encouragement (Wang 1982). Overall, minority parents' expectations of schools and education centre round the very important notions that schools should offer 'equality of opportunity', and should be able to help their children acquire skills and credentials, to accept cultural difference and diversity as legitimate processes, and to respect all the children equally. However, as further discussions will show, it is not surprising that schools have had problems in satisfying these expectations.

Satisfactions and dissatisfactions

Despite the anxieties expressed by both Caribbean and Asian parents about education, in the few studies that have actually sought the views of parents, most have indicated an overall satisfaction with their children's education (Dosanjh 1969, Rex and Tomlinson 1979, Norburn and Wight 1980, Tanna 1981). The researchers have suggested that this finding might be explicable in terms of the colonial educational background of the parents, which meant they lacked knowledge about the school system, and the failure of schools to explain their practices adequately. As Tanna commented of the ten Gujerati Muslim families she interviewed in Lancaster:

> parental lack of understanding is perhaps most clearly indicated by their inadequate knowledge of what exactly their children were learning and how they were taught.

> (Tanna 1981, p.36)

Minority parents have always had to rely more on schools and teachers to inform them about school processes. Indigenous parents, although they may have left school at the minimum leaving age, at least have the advantage of having been through the school system, and have some working knowledge of its intricacies. In the absence of adequate information, many parents perforce may have to be 'satisfied'. There is some evidence (see Chapter Five) that minority parents have been reluctant to admit their lack of knowledge to schools, and some of the supplementary schools now provide information about state education and counsel parents.

To illustrate minority parental views of education, their satisfactions, dissatisfactions and confusions due to lack of knowledge, several research studies are summarised below. They are: firstly, a study in Handsworth, Birmingham, which compared the views of West Indian, Asian (mainly Indian) and 'white British' parents (this study had been reported in Rex and Tomlinson 1979 and Tomlinson 1980, 1981); secondly, a series of small-scale studies undertaken by Ghuman; and thirdly, parental interviews recorded for a study of multi-ethnic schools currently in progress.[2]

The Handsworth study

As part of a research study enquiring into the housing, employment and education of 395 West Indian, 263 Indian, 42 Pakistani and 400 white British heads of households in Handsworth, those parents who had children at school were asked their views on education. The minority parents had all been educated overseas and had limited knowledge about how schools worked, particularly the mysteries of curriculum and examinations, but they demonstrated an eagerness for their children to take advantage of educational opportunities which they had never had. There was little evidence of parental apathy in this study. Most parents were intensely interested in their children's education, even if they had not had much contact with schools. Indeed, there was reluctance on the part of some (mainly Asian) parents to 'interfere' with what was felt to be the school's expertise; 80% of West Indian, 70% of Asian and 88% of British parents had paid a recent visit to their child's school, although many of these visits were on parents' evening or open day — which may not be the best times to establish much contact with teachers. West Indian and Asian parents were more likely to be working longer hours and doing shift work than British parents in the area, making it more difficult for them to visit schools. The British parents' views of schools were, as might be expected, influenced by their own limited schooling, and they were less willing than the minority parents to accept what teachers told them about school and their children's progress. The West Indian and Asian parents demonstrated a greater reliance on teachers' opinions, and on what they were told by teachers about schools and the process of education.

Table 1 below, illustrates reasons the parents gave for satisfaction and dissatisfaction with their children's schooling. 440 parents said they were satisfied, as against 105, who were, occasionally quite vociferously, dissatisfied.

Table 1: Parental satisfaction and dissatisfaction with school

Satisfied because:	W.I. %	Asian %	British %
Children doing well/good reports	77	56	64
Good teachers	11	11	22
Regular schooling	5	16	6
Happy at school	4	8	—
Not held back by coloured children	—	—	4
Other	3	9	4
	100%	100%	100%
Dissatisfied because:	W.I. %	Asian %	British %
Held back by coloured children	4	14	48
Teachers no good	16	19	4
Low standard of education	22	14	19
Poor teaching methods	22	11	15
Poor discipline	4	18	7
No encouragement for slow learners	16	3	—
Didn't get school of choice	4	4	—
Other	12	17	7
	100%	100%	100%

If children get good reports, appear to be doing well and have 'good teachers, all groups of parents view school with some satisfaction. However, the minority parents did perhaps place more faith in the phrase 'doing well' and on the comments of teachers. There is the possibility that teachers can give good reports, and encourage basic literacy and the use of English language at school, without necessarily keeping to a 'standard' similar to that of non-multiracial schools, or producing the 'results' the parents hope for. There was some confusion, particularly amongst Asian parents, about the difference between 'O' level and CSE, and the appropriate age to begin studying for these courses; and there was insufficient appreciation of the fact that a 2-year 'A' level course was the normal route to higher education and professional jobs. More British than minority parents expressed satisfaction because of 'good teachers', and it was interesting to see what parents meant by this. All groups had in mind teachers who got down to the business of teaching literacy and numeracy at primary level, and subjects leading to examination at secondary level. The minority parents preferred teachers who were strict and 'pushed' the children, but who were also kind. When referring to discipline, both West Indian and Asian parents defined it as a firm controlled environment where it was possible to get on with the business of learning rather than punishment. Minority parents also wanted teachers who were non-racist. They were well aware that schools reflect the wider society and that teachers can carry racist attitudes into the classroom. One West Indian mother said that she had been told her children were 'not fit to clean Enoch Powell's shoes'.

A minority of all groups of parents were dissatisfied with their children's education and viewed schools with some dismay. The British parents particularly were worried that their children were 'held back by coloured children', although there has never been evidence to support this view. Interestingly, a few West Indian and Asian parents took this view as well. Some members from all the groups were critical of what they saw as a low standard of education, compared to other schools they knew of, and also criticised teaching methods, curriculum content and discipline.

The West Indian and Asian parents were aware that their children would be at a disadvantage in education if they did not acquire fluency in the English language; but only a quarter of the Asian parents and three West Indian parents thought their children had had difficulty with language on starting school. Asian parents were aware that special language help was available for their children, either at a centre or at school; but West Indian parents who spoke creole in the home used it as any regular linguistic system, and did not see such use of dialect as impeding their children's progress at school. They expected schools to teach and improve on standard English. A quarter of Asian parents reported sending their children to a mosque or temple school for instruction in mother tongue and religion, and felt quite strongly that this was important to keep their children in contact with their own culture. On the other hand, West Indian parents were ambivalent about the idea of promoting a West Indian or 'black' culture. Only a few reported sending their children to the black holiday school run locally by a group of black community workers. They viewed the introduction of 'black studies' or cultural programmes in schools with some suspicion. Some parents were influenced by their own educational background which had stressed European history and achievements, and wanted their children to 'learn about Britain'. Others though that time spent away from 'ordinary' subjects and acquiring the credentials to succeed in British society was time lost. As one parent put it, 'there ain't no "O" level in black studies yet'.

In the Handsworth study, an analysis of parental 'satisfaction' by school, showed that at two of the secondary schools in particular minority parents were more likely to express satisfaction, while at two other schools more dissatisfaction was expressed. Thus, some schools do appear to be able to meet the expectations of minority parents more easily than others.

Three studies of Asian parents
Ghuman, who has consistently deplored the stereotyped use of the term 'Asian' and the level of ignorance in schools about Asian cultures and communities, has undertaken several small-scale research studies of different Asian communities which are extremely valuable for teachers wishing to inform themselves.

In an article on Bhattra Sikhs in Cardiff (Ghuman, 1980a) he describes interviews with 20 Bhattra male heads of households, 12 of whom were skilled workers or shopkeepers, 6 unskilled or unemployed. The interviews were designed to draw out views on marriage, family, education, and the 'British way of life'. Of the three major Sikh groups in Britain – Jats, Ramgharias and Bhattras – the Bhattras are, according to Ghuman, the least-known group, and in the Punjab are considered a low-status group. The men he interviewed were aged between 25 and 65, had been in England for more than 15 years, but still had a poor command of English. From the interviews, Ghuman concluded that the Bhattra Sikhs as a community appeared to be more tightly knit and traditional in their outlook than other groups. He speculated that the Bhattras may want to adhere to their religious and social way of life to compensate for their low status, but he also noted that their perceptions of their white neighbours were very negative. The whites were perceived as morally lax and there was no desire to mix with them. The group's view of the education system was also very negative.

> The community, being ultra-conservative, actually feels its identity and way of life threatened by the schools. The Bhattras feel so unfamiliar with the British education system that the parents do not in any way participate in the education process. (p.314).

Bhattra children leave school at the minimum leaving age, do not go into the 6th form, and do not participate in extra-curricular activity. However, the Cardiff schools the children attended had taken no interest in Bhattra history, language or religion and had made no attempt to explain an unfamiliar education system; and there had been no effort on the part of schools to allay fears about 'anglicisation' and the threat to the Bhattra way of life. Bhattra Sikh parents thus represented an extreme position, of dissatisfaction with (Welsh) education, lack of knowledge, and non-communication with schools. The views of the Bhattras, as Ghuman points out, contrast sharply with those of other Asian groups who mostly, despite some dissatisfaction, view education in a positive light and as a means to occupational and social improvement.

In a study of 40 Jat Sikh Punjabi families living in London, Nottingham, Derby, Leicester and Bradford, Ghuman solicited the views of 30 fathers and ten mothers on school curriculum, uniform, discipline, teaching methods, co-education, prejudice, the employment of Punjabi teachers and English schooling in general (1980b). Thirteen of the parents were graduates but ten had had no education; while they had mostly held non-manual or skilled jobs abroad, in Britain only nine were employed in professional or non-manual jobs. Overall, Ghuman found that these parents expressed satisfaction with English schooling, valued education for its own sake, and expressed faith in teachers and their professionalism – although the middle-class families had more anxieties about academic achievements. There were, however, some important reservations: while corporal punishment was deplored, discipline in schools was considered to be lax, homework was insufficient, and there was criticism of co-education. Over half the sample wanted single-sex schooling. As one father said, 'There should be a choice open to parents. In a democracy it should be possible to choose'. The parents wanted their children to be taught Punjabi and have some knowledge of cultural traditions, but felt that this was the job of the community. Less than half wanted 'mother-tongue' taught in schools – they felt that the Gudwara school on Sunday should teach the language.

The parents exhibited considerable ignorance about what actually went on in school; 58% had no views on the curriculum or could not discuss it in any meaningful way. Lack of knowledge meant that some parents were driven to rely on hearsay and opinion – not a good basis for genuine understanding. As one father (a bus driver) remarked:

> I can't say much on this topic as I am not knowledgeable about these issues. However, in my opinion there is no 'routine' work, and as a consequence children cannot add up. Some teachers pass time and do not teach children whole-heartedly.

(Ghuman 1980 b, p.125)

The parents in this sample felt that the employment of more Punjabi teachers in schools would help their children 'build up positive self-concepts of themselves through identification', and would help to teach Punjabi language and culture; but they also held white teachers in high esteem and valued the contribution teachers made towards making school a pleasant place for their children.

The third study undertaken by Ghuman involved 30 Bengali families in Cardiff, 11 Hindu Bengalis from India, and 19 Muslim Bengalis from Bangladesh (Ghuman and Gallop 1981). The level of education, command of English, occupational position, and housing circumstances of the Hindu parents were superior to those of the Muslim parents, although on average all the parents had been in Wales for 15 years. The Hindu migrants came from professional families in areas well provided with secondary education, they themselves had professional qualifications and spoke good English. They had, in turn, high aspirations for their own children, and expectations that they would do well in education. The Muslim Bengalis, coming from areas where educational facilities were poor had a much lower level of schooling, felt they had had little parental help with their own schooling and, even with the best intentions, could not provide much support for their own children. One father said, 'as I spend all night in the restaurant, I sleep all day and the child is at school; I don't have enough time to spend with my child.'

Another parent indicated that lack of knowledge about education in Britain inhibited him from even trying to help his children:

> Because we do not know exactly what or how they teach in schools here we cannot help our children at home. Even if we want to coach them at home we don't know how. Most of the mothers don't know English so cannot help the children with their studies.

Muslim parents tended to express more dissatisfaction with schools, particularly over religious and mother-tongue teaching, dress, food and co-education. They felt that their Islamic way of life was threatened if schools would not relax rules and change regulations. One or two parents had considered sending their daughters back to Bangladesh rather than allow them to 'wear skirts and be educated with boys.' The parents appreciated the difficulties involved in teaching Bengali in schools (it is interesting to note that the schools their children attended taught Welsh, so that the children were tri-lingual – in English, Welsh and Bengali!) and in teaching Isalm as well as Christianity. They made their own community arrangements, but they still expressed a desire for schools to do more. The Hindu parents were less likely to object to co-education than the Muslims.

Both Hindu and Muslim parents expressed overall satisfaction with their children's education, mainly centred on the positive attitudes and professionalism of the teachers. They felt the teachers were 'dedicated' and racial tensions and discrimination were absent. Muslim parents exhibited less knowledge and active interest in their children's education than Hindu parents, but Hindu parents felt overwhelmingly that the influence of the home was more important than that of the school.

Northern School

As part of a longitudinal study[2] of children attending 20 multi-ethnic schools in four areas of England, one school was visited during a series of interviews which the school had arranged with minority parents. The school, with 70% minority pupils – mainly of Asian origin – was remarkable in that staff were painstakingly beginning to explore in practice what the rhetoric of 'multicultural education' and 'home-school links with minority parents' really might mean. As part of a programme of curriculum development and community co-operation, meetings had been arranged with different ethnic groups. The head wrote in 1982:

> It is anticipated that members of staff will meet with representatives . . . of the Moslem, Sikh, and West Indian communities. Interpreters will be present and social and other workers will help to bring as many people as possible. Parents will be asked what *they* expect from the school and what role *they* see the school as playing . . . we should know what our parents consider a good education.

The meetings, advertised by letters taken home by pupils, were in fact attended by only small numbers of parents. Nine Sikh fathers and a Sikh social worker attended the meeting for Sikh parents; ten fathers, three mothers and a local Imam attended the Muslim parents evenings; and five West Indian parents and a West Indian youth worker attended the meeting for West Indian parents. The parents informed the staff that several of their friends who would have liked to attend were on shift work. An interpreter was required for the meetings of the Muslim and Sikh parents.

The issues raised at these meetings illustrated vividly the overwhelming concern of the Asian parents with cultural issues (concern with examination passes taking second-place in the discussions), while West Indian parents were more concerned with education as a credentialling process. None of the parents demonstrated much knowledge as to what the school actually taught, or about assessment and examinations.

To open the discussion the head invited parents to express their views of the education offered in the school and to talk about any anxieties they might have. The Muslim and Sikh parents immediately raised issues concerning the education of girls (particularly P.E., swimming and clothing), religion, mother-tongue teaching and food, and the possibility of the LEA opening a single-sex school. One father said:

> What we want for our daughters is a basic Islamic training – they must cover themselves modestly – we are worried that our girls get much Western influence.

He produced a set of cuttings from *The Daily Telegraph* reporting arrangements made by Bradford LEA to accommodate Muslim and other ethnic minority community practices and asked why similar arrangements could not be made in his LEA. The Head had to explain the constraints placed on her by the LEA, and in the subsequent discussion the parents agreed that there was a need for compromise; they were willing to compromise over particular issues if they could see the school making similar compromises: one parent pointed out that in response to school complaints, 'we have cut down on the time our children spend at the mosque school.' The Asian parents were in favour of mother-tongue teaching in schools, but not in place of other lessons (they pointed out that their children mainly spoke three languages anyway); would prefer their children not to take part in extra-curricular activities, including sport, that took place after school; and were critical of school discipline, which they felt did not encourage children to respect adults. One parent complained that 'the State is taking away the rights of parents', and feared that this would 'encourage communism, which we do not want here'.

The Asian parents did not spontaneously raise issues concerning curriculum or examinations. When the head mentioned the phrase 'equality of opportunity' one father remarked that there was no equality in England, but it transpired that he was referring to immigration laws concerning the entry of fiancées into Britain. They agreed that passing exams and possibly going into further or higher education was a good thing, although one Sikh father said 'with all the unemployment we ask ourselves whether it is worth them staying on to study'.

The West Indian parents focused their discussion on the aims of education, and the ways of overcoming failure. They regarded education as a 'good' which their children ought to take advantage of. As one mother remarked:

> I send them to school to be better than me; the education is free, it's up to them to take advantage of it.

Another mother said she encouraged her children because if they returned to the West Indies they would find a job easily – 'English education is highly regarded there'.

While the head expressed concern at the low achievement of West Indian pupils in public examinations and stressed how much the school wanted to improve this situation, the parents were worried that the school could not teach them successfully – but opinion was divided as to why this happened. Poor discipline was held to be a factor, although in fact the school is a remarkably friendly and well-disciplined place. One father said, 'you make too many allowances, I send my kids to school to be taught in a disciplined way'. But while agreeing that discipline was stricter in the West Indies, the parents said they did not necessarily support the use of corporal punishment. They felt it was important to make this point as they were aware that West Indian parents were often stereotyped as 'all' wanting corporal punishment. The parents felt that in the West Indies there was more individual contact between parents and teachers, and teachers had high expectations. They said parents asked the advice of teachers more, and there was more private tuition offered if a child was failing in a particular subject. They did not feel that dialect interfered with their children's learning, although one father though West Indian children had more problems 'expressing themselves on paper'. They did not think their children had identity problems, and were not in favour of any curriculum change from 'ordinary subjects'. While the West Indian parents appeared more conversant with subjects taught in secondary schools than Asian parents, they were not too clear about the nature of examinations. One father did not realise that 'O' levels were marked by examiners external to the school, and they complained that because they did not understand the teaching methods, they were unable to help their children. Overall, the parents were agreed that because of the worsening employment situation, it was *more* important that their children passed examinations.

A mismatch of expectations

Research into parental views and expectations of school indicates that, overall, minority parents regard English education as potentially good, and that it should allow for the possibility of passing examinations that will enhance employment prospects or allow chances for further and higher education. West Indian parents expect schools to teach their children in a disciplined and orderly manner and find it hard to understand why teachers find this a difficult task. Asian parents expect that more of their cultural traditions will be incorporated into school practices, and that schools will take more seriously the issues which concern them as parents. The parents in Northern School showed that they at least, are willing to make compromises and have positive suggestions to offer.

However, there are considerable problems involved in satisfying these parental expectations. As Chapter Three indicated, teachers' views of minority parents and pupils make it unlikely that they can actually meet parental expectations unless changes take place. There has certainly been, and may still be, a mismatch between parental expectations and what schools and teachers feel they can actually offer minority parents. The basis for this mismatch, however, may ultimately be the existing structures and functions of the education system and its cultural content. Minority parents' satisfaction with the education system — 'it's there for them to take advantage of', as one West Indian mother put it — rests on the post-war liberal ideology that equality of opportunity, or at least equal chances to be unequal, would prevail. But the ending of the tripartite system and moves to comprehensivisation have not increased the possibility of equality of opportunity for large numbers of children. The chances of pupils of manual working class parents being selected and prepared for an academically-oriented education which allows access to higher education have not improved (Halsey *et al* 1980) and inner-city comprehensive schools, which are the schools attended by most minority pupils, do not generally offer a high-status, academic curriculum. It should, perhaps, be noted that the arrival of minority parents did enhance equality of opportunity for many white working class parents, who were able to move to more desirable jobs and areas. The schools attended by minority children are thus likely to contain the residual white 'disadvantaged', and to be geared to lower-level academic work. For teachers to be able to offer 'equal opportunities' with even white suburban comprehensives is difficult. Many inner-city schools are now beginning to realise that they incorporate all levels of ability as far as minority pupils are concerned, and that it is a mistake to regard all the children as 'disadvantaged', but they do not necessarily have the resources or skills to develop these abilities. There are thus likely to be confusions and difficulties in explaining all this to minority parents.

The parents, as research indicates, have always depended more on schools and teachers to explain school processes, and have been handicapped by their lack of knowledge about schools — particularly about curriculum and examinations. But again, it has never been part of the English educational system to explain too clearly to parents why promises of 'equality' were not realisable in practice.

In the late 1960s, some research by Beetham in Birmingham (1967) began a debate as to whether minority parents and pupils had 'unrealistic' expectations and aspirations regarding education and careers. We now know that minority parents are no more unrealistic than white parents in expecting schools to prepare their children for access to jobs or training, and are perhaps *more* realistic in recognising the additional problem of discrimination which their children face. In the current employment situation, minority parents, as the Northern School Sikh father demonstrated, may be as realistic as many other parents in beginning to question the 'point of education'. Overall, though, the present structure of education, with its 'stop-go' policies of comprehensivisation and selection, and the limitations on resources, make it unlikely that the equal opportunities minority parents expect will be realised.

The expectations regarding cultural diversity, and the ability of schools to satisfy these expectations, is another area where misunderstandings may be perpetuated. The multicultural education movement is currently focusing on the curriculum as a target for reform. Changed curriculum practices are expected to ensure both that cultural groups will have an enhanced 'cultural identity' and that white pupils will be taught in less ethnocentric ways. Minority parents have some difficulty in understanding this, and there is little evidence of demand for a changed curriculum in terms of basic subjects, from the parents. The areas where Asian parents would like to see changes – in the education of girls, mother-tongue teaching, religious education, and the negative demand for less participation in extra-curricular activities – are those which teachers may find most difficulty in accepting. The cultural content of the English education system is based on particular beliefs and values which may be distinctly at odds with some Asian cultural beliefs and values. This is not to deny the importance of curriculum change, particularly to decrease ethnocentricism and to combat racist beliefs exhibited by the majority society; but it is important to note that the issue of compulsory swimming lessons for girls may be more important to Muslim parents than multi-ethnic mathematics or anti-racist teaching. The mismatch between schools' and parents' understandings of 'cultural diversity' may continue to be a source of confusion.

Summary
This chapter has attempted to show that whatever the social class of minority parents they exhibit high, 'middle-class', expectations of the education system, and show enthusiasm for schools and for English

education. These expectations are linked to their own colonial educational backgrounds. Minority parents depend more on teachers to explain school processes, and expect schools to be places where both equal opportunity and cultural diversity can be offered. There may be considerable scope for misunderstanding as there is a mismatch between parental expectations and what schools can actually offer.

Notes
1. West Indian parents at a meeting of Northern School parents, February 1983.
2. This study is being jointly undertaken by the Policy Studies Institute, London, and the University of Lancaster. A report is due in 1984. The study, directed by Mr. David Smith and Dr. Sally Tomlinson, is following the progress of all pupils through twenty multi-ethnic schools in Britain. Parents are also being interviewed.

5 Supplementary and Segregated Schooling

> We believe black children aren't getting the best from local schools – they need the qualifications to get the jobs – and we aim to give it to them.
>
> (Mel Chevannes, headteacher,
> Black Arrow Supplementary School)

As we saw in Chapter Four, minority parents, on the whole, regard English state education as a potentially good education, and have high expectations of it. However, the disappointment many parents have experienced, the mismatch of their expectations with what schools actually offer, and the vocal dissatisfaction of a minority of parents, have led to demands from some parents and communities for additional, supplementary, and in some cases segregated, education. This chapter explores ethnic minority initiatives in education, and discusses the contradictions inherent in some of these initiatives. One initial contradiction should be noted: following the 1944 Education Act, the idea that state schools should provide a common and inclusive educational experience for all children has become increasingly accepted; but the existence of additional or supplementary schooling for minority pupils could be seen as undermining the aim of a common education for all pupils. However, it should also perhaps be noted that additional educational provision by parents or community groups now has strong support, as a result of government ideologies of self-help and commitment to increased parental choice and participation in the education process.

Minority initiatives

There is a long history of the provision of supplementary and part-time education by minorities settling in Britain. In the nineteenth century, supplementary schools for Irish children were organised, followed by Jewish, Polish and Italian Schools. A private Chinese school was established in London in 1934 (Ny 1968) followed by part-time schools for Chinese children. A Greek Saturday School, also in London, was set up in 1922; and now, in the 1980s, when a quarter of all Greek Cypriots live in Britain[1] there is a strong commitment to retaining a Greek culture, and part-time schools exist in several cities. The Japanese are probably the most recent group to set up supplementary and private schools; the first opened in London in 1968, mainly to serve the children of Japanese businessmen temporarily in Britain, who will return to Japan and whose children need preparation for competitive Japanese examinations. But the most extensive development of supplementary and additional schooling has been provided by Caribbean, Pakistani and Indian settlers in Britain.

The reasons for the development of supplementary schools are complex, since they relate to the ways different ethnic groups wish to accommodate to the majority society, and the way this society reacts to different groups in terms of discrimination and exclusion. There is, for example, a distinct difference between schools set up to accommodate the children of Japanese or Iraqui business or diplomatic employees, and schools set up for Caribbean or Asian citizens in Britain.

A powerful motive behind the development of Jewish, East European, Greek, Chinese, Indian, Pakistani and Bangladeshi supplementary and additional education has been the desire to retain cultural identity, which in most cases is very strongly linked with the retention of a mother tongue and religious identity. Asian parents in Britain, in particular, face the problem of retaining a linguistic identity which will allow all generations within a family to communicate with each other, while at the same time ensuring that the children can operate in the language of the majority society.

Since the 1960s, additional education – religious, linguistic and cultural – has been offered to Muslim children at mosque schools, and to Sikh and Hindu children in gudwara and temple schools; and there has been a variety of community initiatives at the local level for instruction in mother tongue and culture (see, for example, Coventry 1976). The EEC directive of the mid-1970s, charging member countries with a responsibility to ensure that mother tongue and cultural teaching were available to minority children, certainly stimulated debate in Britain as to how far such teaching should be provided in schools, and how far minority communities should take the initiative. The DES would seem to favour community initiatives. It did not accept that the EEC directive applied in its entirety to 'children whose parents are UK nationals with family origins in other countries' (DES 1981b), but it did accept that there were implications for LEAs. Local Authorities, according to the DES 1981 Circular, should 'explore ways in which mother tongue teaching might be provided, whether during or outside school hours', and noted approvingly that in some areas provision is already made by minority communities. They considered that voluntary self-help schemes to retain language and culture should be encouraged by, for example, offering LEA premises to community groups for their classes. The NUT has also noted that 'voluntary provision already plays an important part in mother-tongue teaching and culture maintenance', but has stressed that co-operation between schools, home and community initiatives is vital, to ensure that minority children did not become overburdened (National Union of Teachers 1982).

The overburdening of pupils attending mosque and temple schools after normal school hours has always worried teachers. The National Association of Headteachers gave evidence to the Rampton-Swann Committee expressing such an anxiety, and pointing out that it was crucial for day and additional schools to understand and co-operate with each other.

Rex, reviewing arguments for and against the provision of minority languages and aspects of home culture in school, concluded:

> The maintenance of minority culture is best left to . . . adult members of the community involved, through supplementary education, unless in rare cases there are schools in which the 'subject' is understood and the place given to it in the curriculum is such that it does not imply inferiority.
>
> (Rex 1981)

While provision of supplementary education by Asian communities may be more related to aspects of cultural diversity, and the maintenance of a cultural identity, the provision of West Indian supplementary education is most strongly connected to the issue of equality of opportunity. As research has indicated, West Indian parents expect schools to teach their children much more successfully than they actually do, and are concerned and anxious that schools do not seem able to help their children pass the examinations increasingly needed for employment in Britain. Stone (1981) has pointed out that supplementary education is common in the West Indies, and the Northern School parents (see previous chapter) stressed that private tuition for children with particular school problems is also usual in the Caribbean.

At the moment, a minority of West Indian parents in Britain have resorted to these kinds of extra-educational provision, but increasingly supplementary education is being regarded as a desirable initiative.

The 'Black Education' movement

There has been sufficient criticism of the education system and enough initiative taken by some black parents, teachers, community workers and academics to be able to speak of a black education movement in Britain. The participants in this movement are united by a belief that schools designed for white, majority children cannot offer equal opportunities to black children, and that supplementary education is thus a necessity, but analyses as to why schools 'fail' black children differ. Some black educationalists point to the inability of urban schools to offer 'equal opportunity' to many white working class pupils, and refer to the poorer resources, less well qualified teaching staff, low teacher expectations, and low level exam courses offered in urban comprehensive schools. As Mel Chevannes has expressed it:

> Some parents believe the system works against blacks and working-class children, and are saying they are not going to take the sludge offered to them – they have higher ideals.
>
> (Chevannes 1982)

This view assumes that educational effort on the part of individual black parents and pupils will have a pay-off in terms of employment and social mobility. A more extreme view is taken by black academics at Birmingham University's Centre for Contemporary Cultural Studies. Carby (1983) has argued that many black parents had rejected the idea that schools could provide equal opportunities for their children by the late 1960s, and believed that state education was pushing young blacks into low-level education to ensure a supply of unskilled labour or an unemployed 'reserve army of labour'. While this extreme view may be held by some parents, and by some young black Britons, the *evidence* to date seems to be that most black parents still look to additional and supplementary schooling to enhance their children's life-chances.

The black parents' education movement has over the past eighteen years taken the form of diverse parents' and community groups, who have acted as pressure groups to campaign for improved education for their children, and have organised supplementary education. By 1965, the North London West Indian Association was becoming anxious about the number of black children sent to ESN-M schools, and in 1970 it lodged a complaint of racial discrimination with the Race Relations Board. The Board reported no evidence of an 'unlawful act', but at a Caribbean educational and community workers' conference held the same year, Coard spoke of the inappropriate way West Indian children were treated in British schools, that could result in them being 'made ESN' (Coard 1972).

Protests about the over-representation of children of West Indian origin in ESN-M schools provided *the* major focus of concern for the black education movement during the 1970s, the over-representation of black pupils in disruptive units also becoming a crucial focus of concern by the late 1970s. It should perhaps be noted that central and local education authorities have never denied such over-representation, nor initiated any enquiries into the area (Tomlinson 1982).

Haringey's black pressure group on education developed in 1977 from a united black women's action group, which had become increasingly worried by the low educational achievement of black pupils (Venning 1983). The group, run as a collective, has consistently pressured the LEA and local schools about low achievement and disproportionate numbers of black children in ESN-M schools and disruptive units, and has campaigned against ethnic record-keeping in schools. The evidence of this group appeared to particularly influence the Rampton Committee's report on the education of children of West Indian origin (DES 1981). One of the most recent actions of the group has been to circulate all primary schools in East Haringey with a letter accusing heads of failing to provide efficient education:

> The teaching of reading, writing, spelling and higher order language skills is your responsibility, and you appear to be failing miserably in that regard with a substantial number of your children, but specially black British children.
>
> (Quoted in Venning 1983)

Unsurprisingly, some of the actions of this group have antagonised schools and teachers.

Black women have been particularly active in setting up parent and community groups concerned with education. Aba Sindi, a black collective in Moss Side, Manchester, developed out of action by women, and now includes a supplementary school and a nursery school. Some local Community Relations Councils have worked with, or set up, parents' groups to pressure LEAs on educational issues. The Redbridge CRC worked with the Black Peoples Progressive Association to produce the report *Cause for Concern,* on the education of black pupils in Redbridge (1978); and Wandsworth Council for Community Relations worked with West Indian parents in 1979 to challenge the right of headteachers in ILEA to suspend black pupils or place them in disruptive units (Hughill 1979).

Black supplementary schools

Actual numbers of black supplementary schools operating in Britain are difficult to estimate, particularly as some are very recent developments and may be operating without central or local educational authority aid or knowledge. The largest number of schools are to be found in the London area. ILEA reported in 1978 that it was giving grant-aid to two supplementary school projects, and recommended aid for a further ten projects. The reasons given for assisting the supplementary projects were that:

– grant aid would respond to, and encourage, parental community interest in the children's education

– the schemes encourage self-help and harness volunteer support

— grant aid would assist the more disadvantaged sectors of inner city society to give their children the same help more fortunate sectors are able to provide
— grant aid would enable the LEA to take a more active part in discussing methods and teaching materials with the sponsors.

(ILEA Report 8689, 1978)

However, grant-aid from local authorities has been criticised by some black academics (e.g. Stone 1981) as a possible way in which spontaneous self-help ideas will be lost, and a more rigid, hierarchic structure of 'alternative education' imposed.

The Home Office has also supplied money for black self-help projects, including supplementary education. Giles undertook a study of supplementary education projects funded under the Home Office self-help scheme in 1978, but his report was not published (it is available on request from the Home Office). Wellum (1981), in a survey of the library needs of pupils attending West Indian supplementary education schemes in London, included an appendix detailing supplementary schools she knew of. Her list included 41 such schools, although she did not claim accuracy or completeness. Research students at the North London Polytechnic worked in five of these schools and a report is available from the Polytechnic (Cronin 1982). Stone, in Chapter Four of her book, *The Education of the Black Child in Britain* (1981), has documented four supplementary schools she visited in London, three being part of wider community projects; and Rex and Tomlinson (1979) described the Saturday and holiday school run by black community workers in Handsworth, Birmingham from 1974. Supplementary schools have been operating in Handsworth, Birmingham and Toxteth, Liverpool from the mid-1970s, and more recently in Wolverhampton, Manchester, Nottingham and other areas where there is a sizeable black population. Supplementary education is thus becoming an increasingly important aspect of the education of black pupils in Britain. To illustrate the rationale for the schools, the meaning of the schools for parents, and the way the schools operate, two examples are described below.

Datchwyng

The Datchwyng Saturday school in Peckham was televised for a BBC programme on multicultural education in 1979, and has also been documented by the headteacher (Clark 1982). The school came into existence as a result of concern expressed by local black parents that their children were not achieving their intellectual potential, and in the belief that some kind of community self-help was needed to supplement inadequate state schooling. Nel Clark has recorded that, arriving in England in the early 1960s, she rapidly became convinced that there were inherent inequalities in the English education system, but that, in particular, the schools did not cater adequately for black children. Black parents, she found, did not know how to express their concern to teachers, but desperately wanted to take some kind of action to help their children:

> My fieldwork started when I arrived in England in 1965. I visited my friends, met many new people, and, being a teacher back home, the conversations always centred on teaching, and what it was like in England. I found that parents were afraid to voice their opinion, felt helpless and frustrated, even though they knew that their children were not getting on well at school. There were cases of children who had come over from the West Indies, and despite high academic ability, were put into a lower class because 'they could not speak English'. These children had later opted out of learning because 'the work was too easy and they were bored'. There were others, too, who were born in England but were not being taught the basics — just play, play — and could not read or write their names. And yet others whose hopes had been daunted because the career which they or their parents had chosen 'was not for them'. I began to become concerned about our children. I was even approached about giving private tuition.
>
> I started to look seriously at what was happening to our children's education, without which their chances of a future would be hopeless. I then considered all the possible things which could affect their performance and looked for ways in which I could help. My first step was to register for a teacher training course, because I could not enter the profession unless I was qualified.I had taught in Barbados for eight years, and had left the Teachers' Training College after one year to join my husband, who was residing here. I was accepted for a course, which I completed in 1973, but was still at a loss as to how I could help the children.
>
> My second step was to form a parents' group, where parents could receive help and information on how to help their children and how to widen their knowledge. In 1974 this group was formed, and at our meetings we discussed various topics — education, housing, welfare, culture and cultural events, health, social and emotional problems, the community and agencies which work with children and parents. One of the projects which the parents decided to focus on was the Community School, which started in 1975.

(Clark 1982, p.122-3)

The school, held on Saturdays, developed with Clark as the only professional teacher, but with parental assistance. Qualified English and West Indian teachers have at times given their services voluntarily, and in 1980, there were 126 children from 56 families attending the school, and an evening session for 14-16 year olds had been introduced. Subjects taught at the school have always included reading, writing, English, maths, art and craft. Science and French have been taught sporadically when qualified teachers were available. No written records of children's progress are kept, but parents have consistently reported an improvement in their children's school work, attitudes to learning, ability to master new skills and concepts, self-confidence and social and emotional behaviour. In 1980, an exhibition of the children's work was visited by LEA teachers and inspectors, but there had been, up to this time, no contact with the schools which the children attended during the week.

Nel Clark is frank about the problems faced by Saturday schools:

> One of the problems which faced us when we started the school was the attitude of some parents who felt that the school was not good enough for their children. Some children felt that five days in school was enough. Many people asked why there were not white children at the school. Some West Indians felt that Black History and Black Studies should be taught. Some parents felt that only qualified teachers should be doing the teaching. Despite these problems the school continues because parents who felt the school was helping their children have continued to give their support, and it was noticeable that the children from these families attended regularly and made more progress with their work than others did. There were also parents who sent their children to the school, but never visited it themselves, nor took an active part, and subsequently the children withdrew. Other children withdrew for various other reasons.
> (Clark 1982, p.125)

Clark attributes the success of Datchwyng school to the continued support of parents, but success must also in a large measure be credited to Clark herself.

Black Arrow School

The Black Arrow School in Wolverhampton has also been documented by its headteacher, Mel Chevannes (Chevannes 1979). It goes beyond the 'supplementary' philosophy of improving children's educational performance and motivating them to learn, although these aims are important. The school came into being in 1977, a time when members of the Black Arrow Organisation, an Afro-Caribbean community group in Wolverhampton, were becoming concerned about the educational performance of black pupils in state schools. As well as aiming to improve basic performance, particularly in English and maths, the school aims to 'increase the sense of community purpose and pride among the borough's Afro-Caribbean families', and 'to provide information about the rich cultural heritage of Afro-Caribbean people'. The school prospectus notes that:

> The School Trustees, to whom the Black Arrow organisation handed over the responsibility for running the school, are strongly committed to the struggle for racial equality and justice in Britain. They believe in the importance of developing a truly multicultural education, and of black people participating fully and on an equal footing in the mainstream of social life.
> (Black Arrow Supplementary School Prospectus 1982, p.6)

The trustees, however, reject any separatist philosophies and 'black Zionist' movements which might lead to educational segregation. The school offers supplementary education on two nights per week to children (of all races) aged 5-15 years. One session is spent studying maths, and another English and social studies. Older pupils are encouraged to bring homework for public examination preparation to school for help, and English and sociology are taught at school to 'O' level. Unlike the Datchwyng school, the staff are all qualified: the head teacher, Mel Chevannes, holds a degree and both teaching and nursing qualifications, while the other staff are all trained teachers with one or more degrees. Chevannes (1979) has pointed out that the school does practice a form of streaming, as some teachers felt they could not cope with mixed ability teaching, and pupils with learning difficulties are particularly separated out for special help. There is a rigorous set of rules which must be adhered to by pupils, and although the LEA makes school premises available free of charge, other finance for the school has to be raised by sponsors and fund-raising activities.

The school uses similar home-school contacts to those practised in full-time state schools. A parents' evening is held once a term and home-visiting is undertaken. An additional contact is an Advisory Service offered by the school. The prospectus notes that,

> Many parents are afraid to admit that they do not understand some of the details of the British education system. For example, the choice of subject or examination in secondary schools can affect a young person's job prospects. If you would like to talk to a teacher in the Black Arrow School about any detail of your child's education, please do so.
>
> (Black Arrow School Prospectus 1982, p.5)

The supplementary school movement has recognised that minority parents might have difficulty in understanding an unfamiliar education system, and has endeavoured to provide the information which, by and large, schools and teachers in Britain have seldom volunteered.

Stone (1981, p.148) has pointed out that the development of Saturday schools within the black community mirrors the Socialist Sunday School image of the late nineteenth-century, which 'offered working-class children the means to foster a self-image based not on therapy or charity, but on hard work, disciplined study, and the will to succeed'. Interestingly, these are 'values' currently being supported by a twentieth century Conservative government. One irony of the 'under-achievement' of black children in British schools may be that many black parents are becoming committed to the kind of academic, rigorous education which is regarded as 'high-status' or élite in Britain and traditionally offered by the 'grammar' and 'public' schools, but which is increasingly being questioned as a suitable education for the majority of white children (Hargreaves 1983).

Black segregated education

The idea that any form of racially segregated education should exist in British schools has always been repudiated by government and by educationists in Britain. The NUT wrote in 1967:

> It hardly needs saying that the Union, and we believe, the overwhelming majority of citizens of this country, would instantly repudiate any pattern of organisation which enshrined the principle of what is usually known as apartheid . . . that is, setting up of separate institutions or school organisations.

> (NUT 1967, p.3)

This attitude has persisted. In 1980, when the Home Affairs Committee was gathering evidence for its report *Racial Disadvantage*, DES officials were shocked by the advocacy of separate black schools by representatives of the Liverpool CRC. An HMI spoke of,

> . . . the extraordinary advocacy of the witness from the CRC of black-only schools. This would seem to be a form of educational apartheid contrary to all we have been doing to build up a multiracial society

> (Home Affairs Committee 1981, evidence p.443).

Nevertheless, the movement of white families from inner cities has meant that *de facto* segregation does exist in many urban schools, and these schools are the focus of some parental complaint. The 'failure' of schools to educate black children successfully has led to demands for official, separate black schools. Worrell, a black teacher, published an article in 1972 in which he advocated the education of West Indian pupils in all-black schools at the primary level, with pupils moving back into 'white' schools when they were academically as well qualified as their peers (Worrell 1972). The West Indian Standing Conference, a group representing all West Indian organisations in the UK, proposed in 1977 that a black school should be set up as a pilot scheme. Such a school, it was suggested, should be centrally funded and inspected by DES, but 'managed completely by black teaching staff with all-black pupils . . . the curriculum would be slightly changed to accommodate the cultural and historical development of black children whose "identity problems" may be causing concern'. (*West Indian World* 1977).

A small number of black community workers also called for black segregated education at a conference meeting to discuss the Rampton Report (Rampton Conference, November 1981). They cited the opening of an independent black school, run by the Seventh Day Adventist religion, in North London, as an indication that black parents favour segregated education. This school was televised for a BBC 2 programme in November 1982, and the headteacher, Orville Woodford, was interviewed (Woodford 1982). The school is run along traditional English 'grammar-school' lines, it is for black pupils only, fees are £700 per annum, and the 23 teachers are black. As one member of staff remarked:

> Staff identify with the children, they don't label black children's stages of development as a 'problem'. White teachers, no matter how sympathetic, are unable to do this.

The school has a uniform, strict rules which must be adhered to, and a 'subject-centred' curriculum. As Woodford noted,

> Black parents don't want black studies or multicultural education – that is for white children; our pupils need to be good at science, history, geography, and at what society thinks of as things of worth – it is like any good grammar school here.

The basis for black segregated education, then, is still a belief that such an education will ultimately help black children to succeed in an 'English' education, and acquire credentials which will prepare them for employment or further education and training in the majority society. The theme of equality of opportunity runs strongly through all demands for black supplementary and segregated education.

Muslim education

The desire expressed by Muslim religious and community leaders, and a number of Muslim parents, for private or state-subsidised segregated education has quite a different base from West Indian desires for segregated education. Muslim parents are increasingly in conflict with a secularised co-educational Western educational system, and have become more vocal, particularly since the world-wide resurgence of Islam after the Iranian revolution[2] in asserting their own community needs and values. There is enormous scope for conflict and misunderstanding over this issue, as Islamic education is based on quite different principles and values to those of English education. In particular, Muslim parents question the materialistic and competitive basis of English education, the individualistic nature of learning, the way girls are educated, the predominance of Christian influence, and the separation of education from other aspects of life. These issues are tied in with a major anxiety which many Muslim parents feel: that their British-born children will move away from their faith, culture and influence. The Union of Muslim Organisations, an umbrella for all

Muslim groups in Britain, has expressed the dilemma facing many parents thus:

> A major worry for Muslim parents is that their children soon begin to adopt English standards and ideas. They start to question not only traditional customs, but religious ideas which seem strangely alien to life in a Western materialistic society. Islam is not something which can be learnt and adhered to overnight, it must be lived, breathed and fostered, it cannot be separated from life itself . . . Most Muslims acknowledge that Britain is a fair place to live . . . but it is hard to judge how possible it is to live as a Muslim in British society as a whole.

(UMO 1975, p.10).

For about twenty years, Muslim organisations in Britain have attempted to explain Islamic education to educationalists and persuade schools to recognise the validity of at least some Islamic ideas on education. The Muslim Educational Trust, registered as a charity in 1964, organised teachers to visit schools to teach religious education to Muslim children and explain Islamic principles to the schools, but it is probably true that for many years schools were unreceptive and have found great difficulty in reconciling English education and Islamic principles. Many schools serving Muslim communities became familiar with arguments over food, dress, P.E., swimming, dance and co-education for girls, and have only recently begun to relax school rules and accommodate to different standards. Few LEAs have gone as far as the Bradford Authority, who have issued comprehensive guidelines to schools on 'provision for pupils of ethnic minorities' – particularly Muslim pupils – which include for example a recommendation that halal meat be available at school lunch-times (Bradford 1982).

Partly because schools were so unreceptive to Muslim principles, the demand for separate Muslim education, as distinct from the religious, cultural and mother-tongue supplementary education offered in mosque schools and private houses, has grown over the last ten years. A working party on the education of Muslim children was set up in 1974, following a conference on Islamic education in London. It presented its first report, *Islamic Education and Single-Sex Schools*, to the DES in 1975 (UMO 1975). This paper set out to explain Islamic principles related to single-sex secondary education, and drew attention to the voluntary school arrangements laid out in the 1944 Education Act, which 'could enable Muslims to have separate schools'. In 1978, the National Muslim Educational Council was set up, and produced a set of papers on education (UMO 1978) which further developed the case for separate state-subsidised Muslim secondary schooling, and the possible creation of a Muslim University in London. Despite advocating separate Muslim education, these organisations have been concerned to avoid the charge of segregation, recognising that Muslim schools might be seen as racially segregated (UMO 1975, p.20), and have stressed that non-Muslims could attend such schools. The most recent development in Muslim demands for control over their own schools has been in Bradford, where the Muslim Parents Association has formally requested that five county schools (2 first, 2 middle and 1 secondary) be reclassified as a voluntary-aided and the heads and school governors replaced by Muslims (Lodge 1983). The move has some support from the Bradford Council of Mosques, whose secretary was reported as saying: 'Parents would support a voluntary-aided Islamic school 100%. The major problem is the education of our girls'. (Lodge 1983, p.10). However, there are some signs that in Bradford, and elsewhere, the need for separate schooling is seen as less important now that state schools are beginning to take account of Muslim cultural, religious and dietary needs. The proposal for separate state schooling for Muslim pupils was also opposed by an association of young Asians in Bradford.

Muslim organisations have also considered setting up privately-funded independent schools – several are already in existence – and have at various times sought funding from Muslim countries overseas. Lodge reported in 1982 that Muslims in Batley, West Yorkshire, had appealed to the Libyan Government for aid to open a private primary school (Lodge 1982). Malik, a community relations officer in Kirklees, has noted the 'considerable discussion and debate on the rise of Independent Muslim Schools in Kirklees and indeed elsewhere' (Malik 1982, p.21).

Muslim desires for changes in the education of their children would seem, at present, to follow a continuum whereby some parents would be happy for their children to remain in existing state schools, providing more recognition was given to Islamic principles, but some, particularly religious leaders, would prefer voluntary-aided Muslim schools. Private Muslim schools are regarded as a last resort. The kind of changes many parents would like to see in state schools have been documented by Iqubal (Iqubal in UMO 1978). He has written approvingly of the Sidney Stringer School in Coventry, where mother-tongue teaching, Islamic studies in single-sex annexes, freedom to withdraw children from Christian R.E. lessons, respect for dress, food and other cultural symbols, all add up to a school which 'takes due regard of the religious and cultural aspirations of [Muslim] children and parents' (UMO 1978 p.28). It is interesting that Iqubal is of the opinion that Muslim 'salvation' does *not* lie in the 'acquisition of professional qualifications or white-collar jobs' in the Western world, but in following Islam and Islamic principles of education.

The DES and some LEAs now find themselves in conflict with the demands Muslim communities are making, and are facing a series of dilemmas. There is no doubt that the 1944 Education Act allows for the creation of voluntary-aided religious schools. Dr Rhodes Boyson announced in Parliament early in 1982:

> The Government fully supports the very valuable part that voluntary schools play in our education system. They provide what many parents want for their children – education in a maintained school but in an atmosphere which reflects their faith.
>
> (*Hansard*, Vol. 18, No. 58, 16 Feb., Col. 128)

The present government is committed to increased parental involvement and initiative in education. However, it is debatable whether government had the Muslim religion or Muslim schools in mind when referring to voluntary schooling. Mrs Thatcher herself was reported in a recent interview as saying that in schools it was the state's job to express certain values and standards 'and these, I would say, are based inherently on Judaism and Christianity' (*The Sunday Times*, 27.2.83, p.34)

Some educationalists and Christian leaders have also expressed doubts about voluntary-aided Muslim schools. P.S. Dosanjh, who carried out the early study of Muslim parents reported in Chapter Four, and is currently a teacher in Birmingham, is of the opinion that Muslim denominational schools would be 'divisive and counter-productive' (Spencer 1982a). The World Council of Churches also published a document in 1982 which noted that any school run for one denomination could be divisive, and used the example of Northern Ireland to illustrate potential conflicts (World Council of Churches 1982). The Islamic education of girls also poses problems for English educationalists, since the whole trust of girls' education in Britain for the past hundred years has been aimed at giving girls parity of opportunity with boys to enable them to aim for any occupation, rather than being educated for a separate sphere of life.

All in all, Muslim community and parental desires, even for educational change incorporating minimum Islamic principles in state schools, poses problems, and the notion of voluntary-aided separate Muslim schools is fraught with great contradictions. This issue probably emerges as one of the most difficult subsumed under the easy phrase 'multicultural education'.

Sikh education

There have also been moves on the part of Sikh communities in Britain to establish separate Sikh schools, in addition to the supplementary education offered in the gudwara, to teach Sikh children religious principles, mother-tongue and culture. Unlike the Muslim communities, Sikh parents who desire separate schooling may be as interested in equipping their children with better qualifications to compete in Western society, as in providing cultural cohesiveness. Helwig, in 1979, documented a debate held in 1970 in Gravesend, concerning the setting up of a Khalsa (Sikh community) school. He described how, after the founding of a Sikh missionary society, two Sikh pupils were 'refused admission to an English school on the basis of thinly disguised discrimination', and the development of a Sikh school was discussed at a meeting of parents and community leaders.

A Sikh teacher in a Gravesend state school told the meeting:

> Most Indian children are sent to the secondary school where they study until the age of 16. They are neither taught with exams in view nor given a real education. The enterprising children, encouraged by parents, may work for the CSE. Since their teachers do not take an interest, most of our children just bide their time until they can work in a factory or some comparable job. A few, who perform outstandingly, are put on G.C.E. 'O' level courses and have the door open to colleges.
>
> (Helwig 1979, p.96)

Other parents gave their views that intelligence tests discriminated against Sikh children, that girls were 'taught that their parents were wrong in not giving them freedom', and that in English schools their children were losing all sense of a cultural and religious identity. One leader told the meeting:

> We should instil pride in our religion and culture. The aim of education is to give identity and pride in one's heritage. The British education system is narrow and only concentrates on teaching students to fit into a Christian world, not a universal world.
>
> (Helwig 1979, p.102)

However, other parents considered that the products of Khalsa schools would not 'fit into English society' and disagreed with separate schooling. In the event, no further steps were taken in the area, although the local gudwara did open a nursery school on its premises. Helwig commented that the Sikhs in Gravesend were seeking a niche for their children which would give them respectability, acceptance and equal opportunities with both Punjabi and English people.

Mukherjee has more recently documented the demand, made in 1978 by Sikh leaders in Southall, for a Khalsa school. The demand was influenced by the sale of a local state school to the Church of England, and the leaders sent money to the local council to buy a school in the same manner. The council returned the cheque with the comment:

> There is a difficulty in showing the difference between a religious school, and a

school which is tied to religion, to language and to race.

(Mukherjee 1982, p.135)

It is ironic after this comment that Lord Denning was subsequently to rule that Sikhs were not a racial group. The Sikh leaders in Southall stated:

> The realisation of a Sikh school is crucial not only for the continuity and survival of Sikhism, but is the only guarantee we can offer to our children of success in a hostile and pervasively racist society.

(Mukherjee 1982, p.136)

However, the community was not successful in setting up a Khalsa school. Some state schools, along with other social institutions in Britain, have been remarkably reluctant to accept the symbols of Sikhism. The turban has persistently been seen as a threat, in much the same way as some teachers regard 'Rasta locks' (Bidwell 1978), and currently the wearing of the Kirpaan (ceremonial dagger) is causing problems in Leicestershire schools (*TES* 11.2.83).

Summary

This chapter has discussed initiatives that some minority parents and community leaders have been making towards providing additional, supplementary, and in some cases separate, education for their children.

As a rather crude distinction, it was noted that while Caribbean parents tend to look to supplementary or segregated education as a means for improving their children's educational chances, Asian parents are more concerned that such education should enhance and develop cultural identity, and give support to parental and community values. Muslim parents who seek to ensure that their children are educated as far as possible in accordance with Islamic principles, are posing a series of problems for educationalists and for government, for which there are no easy answers. This issue demonstrates that the creation of a plural, multicultural society necessitates that the majority society accommodate to alternative values.

However, the distinction between the motives of different minorities in setting up alternative schools should not be pushed too far. Black supplementary or segregated schools, with black teachers and a curriculum which takes account of the children's needs, is probably a powerful force in enhancing a sense of worth and a 'cultural identity'; at the same time, some Sikh parents, while wanting separate schools to support the preservation of their cultural heritage, are also concerned about equality of opportunity.

Notes

1. OPCS 1981. The invasion of Cyprus by Turkey meant that during the 1970s many Greek Cypriots emigrated from the island.

2. Naipaul (1982) has noted that since the Iranian revolution of 1980 and the resurgence of Islam as a proselytising religion, Muslims in many countries have felt more confidence in asserting their community and religious values.

6 Practices and problems

Despite tensions arising from contradictory hopes and expectations between schools and homes, a variety of initiatives is being undertaken to improve minority home-school contacts and to communicate with and involve parents and communities more centrally in the education process. It is now becoming clearer that although a good deal of the improved contact is along familiar lines dating from the 1960s – parents' evenings, parent-teacher associations, home-school and community liaison – new style links are being developed with reference to minorities. These new links owe much to local authority discussion with minority community leaders, and the production, in some areas, of written policy guidelines, as well as to the attempted involvement of more minority parents in educational decision-making.

It is not to be expected, however, that improved consultation and liaison with minorities will necessarily remove tensions which are rooted in the structures of education, nor that the implementation of good practice and new ideas will be easy. It has already been suggested that home-school conflicts may be rooted in the wider social structure, and it may be beyond the scope of individuals and schools to change things significantly. Much depends on the political will and leadership of central and local authorities. It may also be the case that improved practice in one area may create problems in another. For example, the suggestion by the Rampton Committee (DES 1981) that teachers should become more involved in home visiting raises questions concerning the professional role of the class teacher in Britain.

This chapter examines some of the practices which have developed which specifically affect minority home-school relations, and some of the accompanying problems. The development of parent-teacher contacts, home, school and community liaison, the policy initiatives of some LEAs, and the consequences of more minority involvement in educational decision-making are examined; and two important areas – relationships with white parents, and the professional role of the teacher – are discussed.

Parent-teacher contact

Even before the Plowden Report (1967) the need for improved parent-teacher contact was becoming more generally recognised, and 'the question of the mechanisms of contact was more at issue than whether contact was a good thing' (Johnson and Ransom 1983, p.24). The recommendations of Plowden and the EPA action-research projects of the early 1970s provided a stimulus for new thinking about the way parents could be involved in education. However, the most common 'contacts' between most parents and teachers have continued to be through parents' evenings, parent-teacher associations, and written reports.

Parents' evenings and 'open days' have always figured as the most prominent element in home-school contact. Johnson and Ransom reported from their study of 109 parents of secondary school age children:

> It was clear that [parents'] evenings carried the burden of interaction between teachers and parents, and that the content of such meetings and the perceptions of parents about these events were crucial in the relationship between family and school. (p.54)

Rex and Tomlinson found in their Handsworth survey (1979) that for the majority of West Indian and Asian parents the 'parents' evening' was the major contact — however fleeting — between parents and class teachers. However, because of conflicting expectations as to the purpose of parents' evenings, and shortage of time, they do not appear to be satisfactory occasions for home-school contact, particularly for minority parents. In the Handsworth study, some parents reported being 'fobbed off', as they saw it, by remarks that 'he was doing alright' or 'making good progress', only to discover later that their child was not progressing academically as they would have wished. In addition, the evenings can fuel teachers' stereotypes, leading to remarks like: 'it's the parents we really want to see who never come', and 'no wonder the Asians can't speak English if their mothers can't'.

Likewise, parent-teacher associations, despite good intentions, have seldom figured as a satisfactory point of contact between schools and minority homes. The pressure to set up PTAs came originally from middle-class parents, and some schools and teachers were resistant to a movement which they feared might interfere with their professional activities. However, the National Confederation of PTAs has guided the movement in a co-operative and non-threatening direction,

> . . . providing a channel of expression of parent opinion in Britain. Our aim is the development of good relationships between home and school — between every home and every school in the realm.
>
> (NCPTA 1982)

Because the aims of PTAs are to encourage consensus and agreement between homes and schools, they rarely incorporate mechanisms for dealing with conflict. Thus, when the interests of parents and schools do not coincide, PTAs may be of little value.

This inability to deal with conflict may be one reason for the low level of participation by minority parents. A black Handsworth parent, interviewed in 1982, reported:

> I was once on the committee of the PTA, but after a period of two or three years I stopped because it was all very frustrating. Out of 40 or 50 parents, only 2 or 3 would stand up for issues concerning all the children. Also, you have Indians who were looking out for the welfare of their children, whites looking out for their children, but when it came to West Indians they don't seem to know which way they want to turn.
>
> (AFFOR 1982, p.40)

If teachers at PTA meetings cannot handle tensions between parents and if parents feel they cannot openly argue about issues, it is not surprising that minority parents feel PTAs have little to offer. In 1967 the National Confederation of PTAs, the campaign for the advancement of State Education, and the Advisory Centre for Education formed a 'Home-School Council' to 'Conduct research into and spread information about Home-School cooperation'. While these organisations, separately and together, have campaigned over a variety of educational issues, the education of minority pupils and minority home-school contacts have not been a priority. The Secretary of the Home-School Council wrote in April 1983:

> We have not published anything specifically on the approach to multicultural home-school links, except to urge mother-tongue letters to parents.[1]

The Advisory Council for Education has recently focused much more on the problems facing minority parents, publicising research on parents and racism, for example (*Where* No. 182, 1982); but the low level of interest shown by these organisations in the past towards minority parents has been matched by minority parents' lack of knowledge about, or involvement with, the organisations.

School reports, the major form of written contact between home and school, also do not appear to be a satisfactory form of home-school contact for minority parents or indeed any parents, although Marland (1974) and others have discussed ways of improving this form of home-school communication.

Research set up at the National Foundation for Educational Research in 1978 was based on the premise that few parents were satisfied with school reports. One of the purposes of the research is to 'investigate the effectiveness of the school report as a means of communication between school and home' (School Reports Newsletter No. 1, 1979); some consideration is being given to how effective reports are found to be by minority parents, and also to what alternative ways of reporting pupil progress and development to parents are possible (see Goacher *et al.* 1983). At the moment, school policies on reports and minority parents' views of reports are largely unresearched issues, although clearly some schools have taken steps to cater for minorities (see, for example, Finch *et al.* 1980).

Professional liaison

Two developments in home-school contact which have affected minority parents more significantly have been the expansion of professional liaison between home and school, and revived interest in the notion of community schooling – whereby schools become a focal point for local, geographically-determined community education and activity. However, these developments have not been unproblematic. It was noted in Chapter One that in some ways it was unfortunate that minority pupils were entering British schools at a time when models of 'disadvantage' were so popular. The 'disadvantage' model has always been particularly reflected in professional liaison with homes, and in recent ideas of community schooling. In the 1960s and early 1970s, both these developments were based on the premise that disadvantaged sections of the population needed welfare and assistance in solving their 'problems', whether these were material or psychological. The ideology of 'disadvantage' assumed that people were not really capable of defining or solving them themselves, but need paid professionals to help them (see for example Midwinter 1972, p.181, 'we must swiftly breed a teaching élite – a vigilante force who will act courageously and imaginatively [in urban schools]'). However, the 'disadvantage' model has never really fitted the situation of minority groups, and minority communities are increasingly voicing a desire to define their own problems and take their own initiatives. But the problem-oriented 'welfare' approach remains central to the work of a variety of professionals who liaise between schools and minority homes, some of them employed by the educational services and some by the social services. Educational social workers, educational home visitors, education welfare officers, school-based social workers, school counsellors and educational psychologists are examples of welfare experts, called in when 'problems' related to the home are made manifest (for further discussion of this point, see Finch 1984).

Home-school liaison teachers, community education teachers, and 'cultural liaison teachers' (see Little and Willey 1981), who gradually increased in numbers during the 1970s, are less likely to be committed to a 'problem-oriented' approach, possibly because they are trained teachers, and more committed to 'educational' issues; but there is still little research and evidence as to how home-school liaison teachers actually do perceive their role, what activities they engage in, and how they are paid. Birmingham, for example, started the decade with two home-school teachers and ended it with some 60 home-school liaison and 20 pre-school workers, largely funded under Section 11 of the Local Government Act of 1966, and the Inner City Partnership Scheme. Although home-school liaison teachers were not likely to be appointed solely to deal with minority homes, in many urban areas contact with minority parents is implicit in the job – but as yet no 'multicultural' training element is required. Although most of the teachers have a teaching commitment in schools, much of their job is open to negotiation and it is left to the individual's discretion as to how much and in what way she or he interacts with minority groups. This may be particularly problematic if the teacher is 'white British'.

A recently appointed community teacher in Nottingham reported her job thus:[2]

> I teach 50% of the time and the rest of the time I do everything else. It's an odd job – at first you don't think you are working if you aren't in front of a class, but you have to tell yourself just talking to people is part of the job. Parents like to come to school and find someone with time to talk to them – or who will go out to talk to them. I'm getting a 'community' room here – I've already got a desk and filing cabinet. I'll probably get more involved with careers advice and preparing pupils for 'leisure' and I've been visiting work experience programmes – including one at the Afro-Caribbean club here.

Another liaison teacher in the city saw her role as more to do with adult education and liaison with Muslim homes:

> I've organised an evening literacy class for parents and am starting one in the day. We're starting a play-group and I'll get Asian mothers in. I have to be careful when I visit homes, I don't go to Muslim homes on Friday because of the prayers and I do find problems of communicating because of language.

One piece of research which evaluated the work of a home liaison tutor scheme was reported by Finch *et al.* (1980).

A one-year scheme, funded by the MSC and employing four home-school tutors, was set up and evaluated. The major aims of the scheme were to 'make contact with parents and bring them into closer contact with the school system, and to promote better teacher understanding of ethnic minority cultures and religions'. After a year's liaison with predominantly Asian parents, the evaluation of the scheme reported limited but tangible 'results', particularly in that minority parents felt more able to approach schools, and the frequency of contact between home and school improved. The tutors were from ethnic minority groups themselves and could communicate in an Asian language, which may have been a significant factor in the success of the project. The evaluators did report that some schools were unsure of the home-tutor's role, regarding her as 'doing nothing' if she was not in a classroom – a feeling noted above by one of the Nottingham community teachers; and the final report also made an interesting comment on the differences between the role of home-school liaison teachers, and other professionals who 'liaised' with homes:

> Home-school liaison seems a duplication of social or educational welfare only if it is narrowly defined as a 'problem-oriented' activity. If, instead of regarding liaison work as confined to the families of those children who present the school with problems, it is seen as an activity which operates on a broad front to foster home-school relations generally, then it is clearly an activity which no other agency specifically undertakes.
>
> (Finch *et al.* 1980, p.22)

Apart from this study, there is little research providing information as to how parents perceive and react to home-school professional liaison. On the 'plus' side, minority parents may very well appreciate discussion with a trained teacher who actually has time to talk and explain educational processes. Parents may also appreciate the use of extra professional skills in organising language and literacy classes, pre-school play groups and parental activities in school, and may particularly appreciate extra careers or training advice for their children. On the 'minus' side, an extra 'layer' of professionals, even if trained teachers, may distance minority parents even further from their children's class teacher – the person they may actually want to see. Also, the confusion of the work of home-school liaison teachers or tutors with that of other professionals whose work is primarily welfare or problem-oriented may mean that this kind of 'contact' is not fully accepted by parents. Evidence to date, however, seems to suggest that the appointment of home-school liaison teachers is a positive step in the direction of encouraging more contact and communication between minority homes and schools; this issue will be taken up again in the final chapter.

Community schooling

Post-Plowden initiatives, particularly in the EPA 'action research' areas, led, in the early 1970s, to a revival of interest in the notion of community schooling, in which schools were to open up resources to parents, become a focal point for the community and become centres for community education. The complexities of defining what exactly is meant by 'community school' or 'community education' have been succinctly described by Fletcher and Thompson (1980), Fletcher noting that 'at present community education takes a potentially bewildering variety of forms' (p.5). For ethnic minority parents, one form it undoubtedly takes is the provision of supplementary and additional education by the minority communities themselves, the kind of community education described in Chapter Five. However, it is probably true that most schools and teachers think of community schooling as making state schools more responsive to local, geographically-defined communities, and if the local area includes minorities, then these 'communities' must also be taken account of. This definition of community schooling certainly informed the 'experiment in community schooling' set up in Birmingham in 1974 and funded by Van Leer, a Dutch charitable trust. The experience of one of the schools in this project, Tindal Primary, has been the subject of a BBC TV programme ('Multicultural education 1980'), and is reported in Twitchen and Demuth (1981, Chapter 3). During the six years that the school was part of the Van Leer project, community rooms at the school were designated both for adult and for 'community' use – pre-school groups of mothers and children, ESL classes for Asian parents, meetings for self-help organisations, and dress-making and keep-fit classes. A home-school liaison teacher had been employed at the school before the project began, and she organised systematic home visiting and regular meetings between liaison staff and the class-teachers. As the school served a geographical area containing Indian and Pakistani families, much of the community liaison programme included liaison with minority homes and parents. A mother-tongue support group was set up, and the provision of mother-tongue teaching, taught after school hours by volunteers, became a major new activity.

> The support group was set up when a cross-section of people, particularly those representing the Asian community, were invited to discuss how the school might respond more sensitively and effectively to the needs of children from Asian homes. It was quite obvious that the overwhelming concern was for the provision of mother-tongue teaching . . . in no time at all we had classes in Urdu and Punjabi for 50 children.
>
> (Twitchen and Demuth, p.32)

The Tindal Association for School and Community was also set up during the life of the project; this is 'an independent organisation based on the school, with a cross-section of elected members including parents, residents, school staff and representatives from voluntary and statutory organisations' (p.33).

The headteacher of Tindal noted, in his comments on the project, that the attempt to make schools more responsive to the community could not be undertaken without facing up to the conflicts of values and interests which were implicit in such an undertaking. In particular, he noted the dilemma of moving into areas of possible conflict with the local authority — such as happened over the issue of mother-tongue teaching on the curriculum; and he also remarked:

> The crunch has to come, too, in that we have found ourselves, on more than one occasion, in a position where we have been asked by the parents and the community to do certain things — or re-adjust our priorities in a particular way . . . and we have been unable to do this.
>
> (p.32)

There are limits on the extent to which schools can actually respond to community wishes, or change to accommodate alternative values; but there are undoubtedly many schools which, despite confusions about the concept of community schooling, *are* attempting to make schools and school activities meaningful to local communities. The head of a Rochdale Primary, a mainly Muslim, school, described his community links thus:[3]

> We have links with the Mosque, religious leaders visit in the day and I invite them to parents' evenings — parents want their children to know about Islam as part of their schooling. We have a mothers' and toddlers' group, and organise talks on things like 'home safety' with interpreters. Parents can come to school at any time, they can go into the classes, help as 'aides', talk to the teachers, and two mornings a week I have an interpreter here. We send also letters home in Urdu. We don't want to make the school a mini-Pakistan, but we do want the children to see images of themselves, and successful images of minority people, represented in school. We invited parents to help on our curriculum development committee — they weren't a lot of use because they didn't know much about it, but they could see we didn't finish at 3.30 and cared about what their children learned.

This head recorded one problem which frustrated the teachers — that of understandings of time:

> Parents put themselves down to be 'aides' for a particular class, then didn't turn up on time or came the next day.

The experiences of most schools which have attempted to respond to the needs and wishes of minority communities has increasingly demonstrated that the 'disadvantage' model is inappropriate. Despite the undoubted social and material disadvantages to be found in urban areas, minority communities do not necessarily consider themselves to be disadvantaged people, in need of what Jackson (1980) has described as 'organisation by professionals'. Increasingly, minority communities are demonstrating that they can articulate their own problems and needs, and attempt to deal with the resulting conflicts and tensions.

Home, school and community contact and liaison is thus coming to be defined on a broader basis than simply the old-style links which have been central to the development of home-school relations in the past.

Policy initiatives

A major initiative in home, school and community relationships over the past few years has been the scrutiny by local authorities of the educational services they offer to ethnic minorities, and their involvement of community representatives in discussions as they draw up new policies or guidelines. As one chairman of an educational services committee remarked:

> For the past twenty years we have been sitting in County Hall identifying the views of the Asian community. In the last two years we've gone out to talk to them, and found they had completely different views from those we perceived.
>
> (Makins 1982)

Although it took some twenty years to recognise that improved contact and communication with minority homes was a matter for wide-ranging and coherent LEA policy rather than simply for professional liaison, by 1981 most authorities with significant numbers of ethnic minorities had appointed 'multicultural' advisers and were giving serious consideration to home-school consultation. Some ten LEAs were also in the process of consulting with minorities before producing written guidelines to assist schools in their dealings with minorities — and minority parents in their dealings with schools. The city of Bradford, with a fifth of its school pupils coming from (mainly Asian) minority homes, has been in the forefront of attempts to evolve a comprehensive policy which would explain and safeguard the rights of minorities, including educational rights. The intention has been to draw up educational policies which would be clear and unequivocal — schools and teachers would have guidelines for putting LEA policies into practice. The draft guidelines drawn up for schools in 1982 stated:

> Bradford council is committed to a policy of taking whatever steps are necessary to develop harmonious relations between all ethnic minority groups which make up the population of the district . . . provision for ethnic minority children is part of the provision for all our children.
>
> (Bradford City Council 1982, p.1)

The guidelines go on to note that, 'it has long been the policy of the Directorate of Educational Services to develop and reinforce relationships between home, community and school', and, 'It is important that minority group parents should, as should all parents, become familiar with the nature of the schooling that their children are receiving, and be able to discuss difficulties' (p.2). The guidelines were developed after discussions with community groups – religious education being a particular focus for debate – and the authority recognised that there might be tensions and value conflicts in the different expectations that the community, parents and teachers hold about schools:

> A clash of aims in the education of the child may undermine the opportunity of the child to take full advantage of the education system. (p.2)

The document set out the rights of parents as laid down by the 1944 and 1980 Education Acts, and recommended that this information should be included in booklets prepared for parents, translated into minority languages where necessary. It also incorporated recognition of the particular needs of Muslim and Sikh children – religious education, mother tongue teaching, physical education, clothing, food and the recording of names. It has already been noted in Chapter Five that greater familiarity with the 1944 Education Act, and the provision it made for voluntary-aided schooling, led community and religious leaders in Bradford to press for separate, voluntary-aided Muslim schools. Although this issue has not yet (May 1983), been fully resolved it is a good illustration of the way in which genuine consultation with minorities can elicit views which may not be compatible with the current, Western education system.

The neighbouring authority of Kirklees also set out, in the early 1980s, to produce a set of recommendations to guide the local authority services in their relations with minority communities, but they felt that, while local authorities could make efforts, a national policy commitment was necessary to ensure that minority communities were really listened to and their interests safeguarded:

> There is little hope of achieving, by preconceived methods, equality of opportunity, tolerance and respect for cultural diversity if these are not recognised as desirable by the nation as a whole – a national strategy is required for both policy and resources.
>
> (Kirklees 1981, p.1)

The authority held discussions with minority communities, and noted that, 'strong foundations had been laid in linking the education services to those members of the minority community who have particular interest in its development' (p.4). Development of parent-school contacts had, to date, 'largely been a matter for individual schools' (p.5). Asian mothers' groups, ESL teaching, home visits by teachers and two specially appointed home visitors, and the translation of school notices, were cited as examples of good practice; but a summary of recommendations included reference to the need to develop a proper framework, both to encourage minority group involvement with education, and as a context for home-school links.

Authorities who worked during the 1970s to provide 'support' for minorities may now, in the 1980s, be accepting that equal discussion and debate could lead to more genuine minority involvement with education, but may equally be finding some difficulty in actually putting this aim into practice. The city of Coventry, with 18% of its pupils from minority homes, was one of the first LEAs firmly to commit itself to 'provide an education service which is fair and responsive to the needs of the multicultural community and minority groups' (City of Coventry 1976, p.3). The city had been developing general community education programmes from the early 1970s (Benington 1977), and although the focus of these programmes was initially on 'disadvantaged' pupils, they expanded to involve work with ethnic minority parents and communities. The authority also committed itself early on to increasing the representation of minority group parents on Boards of Governors of schools (City of Coventry 1976, p.5). In 1977 the LEA established a Minority Support Service to 'help meet the changing needs of minority groups in the school system', and this service included the appointment of three welfare officers to act as a liaison between homes and schools. One of these appointments was specifically intended to be responsible for young Asian girls. However, the city may be finding some difficulty in moving away from 'old-style' links and in actually seeking to involve the minority communities as partners. A working party, set up to review the future of post-primary education in the city to the end of the century, did not apparently include any representatives from minority groups, nor did it receive evidence from the minority communities (City of Coventry 1983).

Two education authorities whose commitment to minority community involvement has extended to relatively elaborate consultation are those of Berkshire and Inner London Education Authority. In both these areas concern to inform parents and protect their rights had been extended to the discussion with minorities of their views as to how the education system may contribute to 'racism' in society and perpetuate inequality of opportunity for minority pupils, and how this situation can be remedied. Berkshire in 1981 set up a Committee for multicultural education, chaired by the Director of Education, which produced a discussion paper, *Education for Equality* (1982). The paper urged that schools and teachers should adopt perspectives emphasing 'equality' rather than integration or diversity, and that codes of practice for schools and teachers be worked out. The committee noted that there were many practical questions to be asked and answered before perspectives based on equality could become a reality. Among these questions were:

—what formal arrangements could be made for consultation between the LEA and community organisations?

—what steps could be taken to increase the representation of Afro-Caribbeans and Asians on boards of school governors and other committees?

—what arrangements could be made for allocating funds to schools and classes run by minority community associations?

—what arrangements could be made to increase mutual understanding between schools and parents and help schools deal with issues of equality and racism?

(Berkshire 1982)

Seventeen minority organisations were represented on the Berkshire committee: the Slough Islamic Trust, the Hindu Cultural Society, the Slough and District Standing Committee of Asian Organisations, the Rajasthan Welfare Society, the Apollo Club, the Reading Parents' Asian Group, Reading United Ethnic Minorities, the Muslim Welfare Association, Anjam Ghubaman – E – Rasool, the Indian Welfare Society, the West Indian Peoples' Association, the Pakistan Parents' Society, the Indian Workers' Association, the West Indian Women's Circle, Gudwara Singh Sabha, and Ramgarhia Sabha. The number of organisations that made themselves available for consultation indicates the level of minority parental and community interest in becoming involved in decision-making about the education of their children; but difficulties were experienced in reconciling different views from different groups.

The ILEA is the authority which has gone furthest in attempting to involve minority communities in educational decision-making, working on the assumption that in the past, minorities have suffered from policies and decisions which they had no hand in shaping. The authority produced a policy statement on multi-ethnic education in 1977 and a progress report on the working-out of policies in 1979. Home, school and community links and the involvement of minority communities have always figured as a major priority. For example, by 1979 ten interpreter-translators had been appointed to work in the field of home-school relations with non-English speaking families; the Lambeth 'whole-school' project was in operation – designed to help schools respond to the needs and requirements of minority children; and a community liaison project was operating in Brixton primary schools to develop better home-school understanding (ILEA 1979).

In 1982 and 1983, ILEA held consultations with a wide variety of community and parents' groups, but the deputy leader of the authority was reported as regretting that, 'there has not been as much feedback from black groups as there should have been' (Spencer 1983). A conference was arranged in April 1983 at which some three hundred community groups were represented, to help the authority work out a multicultural education policy, and a variety of conflicting views and opinions was put forward (O'Connor 1983). There is some evidence that authorities are meeting with a lack of success in their efforts to 'involve and consult' parents. One reason for this may be that minority parents may, in the light of past experience, be dubious as to how far local authorities really are prepared to change.

Minority influence

The problems Berkshire and ILEA experienced when they took steps to involve minority community groups and parents in educational decision-making illustrate two general difficulties about such consultation, and raise questions about the extent of minority influence on the education system. The first problem has to do with the difficulty of deciding what exactly constitutes a 'community', and whether 'community leaders' really do represent the views of all or most of a particular group. This is part of a more general problem of representation, now that urban politics are increasingly influenced by pressure groups, and cannot be discussed in any detail here. However, the issue is important, particularly as scarce resources could be claimed by one group at the expense of another. A second question has been raised by Kirp (1983) in the context of American battles for control of school systems. He asks how far 'moral guilt' on the part of a majority society which genuinely accepts that minorities have been discriminated against in the past, should lead to decisions being taken which are not in the interests of all citizens of a particular geographical locality. This is an especially pertinent question in areas where 'disadvantaged whites' feel they are not getting a fair deal from the authorities. Again, this is an important point to note, although it cannot be discussed in detail here.

At the present time the major question is still whether minorities *can* actually have much influence on educational decisions, and whether the way in which this can most directly occur is by the appointment of more minority representatives to school governing bodies, either as parent or as ordinary governors, and to local authority education committees. It was noted in Chapter One that the Taylor Report (1977) made a specific recommendation that minority parents should *not* be deliberately sought out as governors. However, the Home Affairs Committee (1981) regarded this recommendation as a mistake, and urged the Secretary of State to use his powers under the 1980 Education Act to increase the extent to which ethnic minorities are represented on school governing bodies (Home Affairs Committee 1981, p. xiii).

A few LEAs are also beginning to explore ways in which the 'partnership' recommended by the Taylor Report can be put into operation. Newham, a London borough, has recently decided to co-opt four parent members directly onto the Education Committee, since, in the view of the chairman,

> The education of children is a partnership between the local authority and parents – and it's time we involved them as members of the committee.

One of the four parents is to represent ethnic minority interests and will be nominated by Newham Race Relations Association (Bayliss 1983). However, the increased involvement of minority parents as governors or on education committees does raise again the issue of familiarity with the workings of the education system. Bacon (1978) has pointed out that to be effective, school governors need to be knowledgeable. It may not be enough for LEAs to encourage minority representation on educational decision-making bodies, unless they also arrange for some form of induction or training programmes.

White parents

So far this chapter has concentrated on initiatives being undertaken to improve relations between minority homes and schools, and to extend minority influence in education – and the obstacles which can arise as initiatives are implemented. One particular problem area which is seldom discussed or written about is the relationship between schools and white parents in areas of high minority settlement, and the relations between white and non-white parents.

Many teachers have experienced difficulties in dealing with relationships between white and minority parents, and have worried about the extent to which it is possible to offer a 'fair deal' to all groups. Some urban teachers feel that a focus on the problems of minority parents may somehow divert attention from white 'disadvantaged' parents; and other teachers have come under pressure in handling the – sometimes explicit but more often implicit – hostility that many urban white parents display towards minorities.

These problems are long-standing. There is evidence that from the early 1960s many white parents have expressed dismay at what they regarded as the take-over of 'their' schools by 'immigrants', and this dismay has usually been rationalised by fears that standards were being lowered by the presence of minority children. More recently, the rationalisation has changed to suggest that non-white children are being 'favoured' at the expense of white children. As early as 1963, white parents in Southall protested at the numbers of Asian children entering primary schools in the area, and kept their children away from school. In an unprecedented gesture the then Minister of Education visited Southall in person to reassure white parents that measures were being taken to prevent lowered standards. These measures included a recommendation to Parliament that no school should take more than 30% 'immigrant' children, and that dispersal of these children be effected by bussing (see Rose and Associates, 1969).

Both these concessions turned out to be unworkable, minority intake to schools rapidly rose above the 30% level to make them 'majority immigrant' schools, and bussing was eventually ruled to be racially discriminatory.

Nevertheless, throughout the 1970s many white parents remained antagonistic to the idea of their children attending schools with minority pupils and, as in the USA, 'white flight' from urban areas was partly a flight from such schools. The Select Committee on Race Relations and Immigration, collecting evidence for their 1973 Report on Education, found that Liverpool Councillors were sure that in inner Liverpool a major reason for whites seeking re-housing was to prevent their children being sent, as one man had told a councillor, 'to be educated with coons' (Select Committee 1973, vol. 3. p.557). The school in question was Paddington Comprehensive, which only a year before had been made nationally famous by Eric Midwinter's account of its supposedly successful community activities (Midwinter 1972). One irony of white flight is that schools may then become further stigmatised as being 'all-black', or may succumb to closure or amalgamation as a result of falling rolls. This situation threatened Paddington Comprehensive in the early 1980s, provoking the Liverpool Black Organisation, in its evidence to the Home Affairs Committee for the report *Racial Disadvantage*, to assert that the City Council, 'constantly seeks to close down those schools which significant numbers of black children attend. They seem more concerned to appease white hostility to the creation of so-called ghetto schools than anything else' (Home Affairs Committee 1981, p.610). They pointed out that white parents do not appear to want their children educated alongside non-whites, but at the same time do not want 'all black' schools.

In other localities, it was possible to document during the 1970s the extent of white hostility to minority parents and pupils. Rex and Tomlinson reported from their survey of white and minority parents in Birmingham:

> Among the white parents the feeling was that the presence of black children stigmatised their schools. Even if they were to accept the view . . . that there was no proof that large numbers of black children held their children back (something they were not inclined to believe), the fact that they thought that other people thought that it was degrading to go to an immigrant majority school was a sufficient basis for believing that they put their children at a disadvantage by sending them there.
>
> (Rex and Tomlinson 1979, p.194)

Further evidence from a survey of 491 West Indian, Asian and white parents – examining how parental attitudes and values were likely to affect children (Davey and Norburn 1980), also indicated that white parents were less enthusiastic about multiracial schools than other groups, and 20% said they would take the racial mix of a neighbourhood into account if they moved house.

The assumption that there is a stigma attached to having white children educated with non-white minority children, even temporarily, applies as much to middle-class as to working-class parents. Richards, reporting a recent Nottinghamshire project in which an exchange was organised between an inner city junior school and a suburban primary school, noted:

> After the first week the head of the North Nottingham school received complaints from some parents about the project – objecting to their children mixing with 'these immigrants' from the city centre.
>
> (Richards 1983, p.223)

The hostility to 'immigrants' also extends to any form of positive action being taken to help minorities with their specific problems. Richards also reported that in a Nottingham city centre school where two Section 11 teachers had been appointed to teach ESL and Punjabi, 'the head of the school received complaints and deputations from some parents, vigorously objecting to both these initiatives on the grounds that the "coloured" children were being favoured to the detriment of their own' (Richards 1983).

The reasons for white hostility to non-whites are not difficult to comprehend, and inter-ethnic hostility is not limited to Britain in the 1980s. White parents of all social classes have, by and large, been educated through an ethnocentric curriculum which, even post-war, continued to present non-whites in a stereotyped and derogatory manner, and incorporated beliefs which had been developed over three hundred years of colonialism. The stigma which many white parents feel at having their children educated alongside non-white children has deep historical roots which their own education did little to change. In addition, white parents left in inner city areas often are genuinely 'disadvantaged', and *are* fearful that they will lose out if benefits appear to be offered to one group rather than another. However, many teachers in urban schools are faced with difficult problems in reconciling the views of white and minority parents, and have, to date, received little help or advice in this area. One programme which does face the issue has been recorded for the BBC television series on multicultural education ('Multi-cultural Education', BBC TV 1980; also see Twitchen and Demuth 1981). Here, in a 'racism awareness' workshop, a teacher, Mrs

Thompson, attempts to show how teachers may cope with 'racist' white parents. This is not an easy task. A West Indian mother tells Thompson, 'whites have a problem, and we are landed with it'. However, teachers also have considerable problems in handling the day-to-day realities of parental hostilities and antagonisms.

While solutions to these antagonisms may ultimately lie in political and social change beyond the scope of schools, one novel way through which white and Asian women came into contact, and white hostility was lessened, was reported by Yates (1982). She worked on, and evaluated, a parent-education project in Birmingham at the end of the 1970s (see Chapter Seven). Part of the project included contact with women's groups in the city who volunteered to help produce parent-education materials. In one white group, living,

> . . . in an area in which the respectable working class and tradesmen once lived and which is now predominantly Asian . . . the white women had previously been extremely defensive regarding their racist positions. In many ways they expressed their feelings of being cut off from the larger white community and surrounded by people of strange customs. They also felt their children were receiving a second-rate education because time and expense was being spent on Asians.

> (Yates 1982, p.14)

However, during the project some of the women developed an interest in flowers and plants, and began identifying plants on a plot of wasteland in the area. Several Asian women were seen collecting leaves from the plot:

> They were approached and the group discovered that some of the Asians, particularly those from rural areas, had a vast knowledge of the use of herbs and plants for alternative medicine.

The relationship with the Asian women matured into friendship, and Yates concluded that the white women came to 'respect and learn from the very people who at first appeared to threaten them'.

Class teachers

Any discussion of practices and problems in home-school contact must inevitably come back to a consideration of the role of the class teacher in furthering home-school links. It was noted in Chapter One that the 'end' of home-school contact is generally thought to be the improvement of children's educational performance and attainment, and minority parents certainly see this as a major aim. Liaison with professionals who do not actually teach their children may very well be regarded as an unsatisfactory second-best by some parents. One of the reasons for the continued popularity of parents' evenings may be that they do offer a chance for parents to make at least a brief contact with class or subject teachers. However, several official reports have recently urged that class teachers should spend time visiting homes. The Rampton Committee (DES 1981) suggested both that schools should designate a senior member of staff to co-ordinate school and community links, and that, 'schools should encourage teachers to see home visiting as an integral part of their pastoral responsibilities' (DES 1981, p.80). This can lead to problems and necessitate a re-definition of the teacher's role.

If class teachers do spend time during the school day visiting homes, their professional role as teachers may be affected. There is now accumulating evidence to indicate that effective teaching requires a variety of professional skills (Bennett and McNamara 1979) but a prerequisite is that the class teacher is actually present in the classroom. There is also evidence that between schools there can be a wide variation in the amount of teaching and learning time available; some schools 'waste' more teaching time than others and are less effective as a consequence (Bennett 1979). Parents may want more contact with their child's class teacher, but if it can only be arranged at the expense of teaching and learning time which might affect pupil performance, this form of home-school contact becomes less attractive. Although other teachers could take over, or 'team-teaching' could be adopted, effective teaching and home-visiting by class-teachers may not be compatible. An alternative is incorporating home-visiting into a class-teacher's out-of-school time, which leads to professional problems and redefinitions. One form of contact between parents and class-teachers which was designed to improve pupil performance without affecting teaching time was the 'reading project' pioneered in Haringey and in Rochdale, in which parents co-operated with class teachers in hearing their children read (Hewison and Tizard 1980, Jackson and Hannon 1981). These projects demonstrated that when there are good relationships between parents and class teachers, children learn more effectively; and that parental co-operation can both motivate children to learn to read and teachers to produce more and better reading materials. The Bellfield project in Rochdale tackled the question of home visiting by class-teachers, and suggested that if the NUT policy of allowing all teachers one-fifth of their time as 'preparation' were implemented, class teachers would be able to fit in home visiting (Jackson and Hannon 1981, p.17).

Summary
This chapter has discussed a variety of practices which have developed, or are developing, to improve home-school contact and communication with minority homes, and illustrates that behind the easy rhetoric of 'improved home-school liaison' lie a variety of problems. The more

familiar contacts of parents' evenings, PTAs, and school reports were noted as important, with built-in limitations that could be given some attention. To overcome these limitations a tier of professionals employed to liaise with homes has developed, but the confusion of problem-oriented welfare liaison with educational liaison was noted as a particular problem. The development of community education − defined as state schools attempting to become more responsive to local areas − could be seen as a basis for positive and increased contact with minority homes; but the idea that urban community schools largely serve 'disadvantaged' sectors of the population may affect developments. Policy initiatives by LEAs to involve minority communities in educational decision-making and as representatives were noted, as these 'new-style' links are attempting to define minority parents as 'equal partners'. The problems of relationships between white parents and multiracial schools and between white and minority parents were discussed; and finally, the chapter reiterated that the end of improved home-school contact was generally seen to be the improvement of pupil performance, and raised questions concerning the professional role of the class-teacher in home-school contacts.

Notes

1. Private communication from the Secretary of the Home-School Council, April 1983.
2. Interviews with Nottingham Community Education Teachers, March 1983.
3. Visit to Sparrow Hill School, Rochdale, 12.5.82.

7 Pre-School Provision

The issue about which educationists and ethnic minority parents are in the closest agreement is that of pre-school provision. There is a general consensus that the care and education offered to minority children before compulsory schooling is of crucial importance to the educational development of the children, and equally, there is a consensus that care and provision are inadequate. The Select Committee on Race Relations and Immigration heard evidence for their 1973 report that:

> A contributory factor in the underachievement of minority group children in our education system is the inadequacy of pre-school provision.
>
> (Select Committee 1973, vol. 3, p.438)

And similarly, the Home Affairs Committee noted in 1981 that:

> It is not only the case that there is a particularly heavy demand for under-five facilities from the ethnic minority communities, it is also the case that they would benefit particularly from an expansion of such facilities.
>
> (Home Affairs Committee, 1981, p.xii)

The Rampton Committee, in summarising their 81 recommendations on the education of children of West Indian origin, placed their seven recommendations on pre-school provision first, particularly recommending that:

> All local authorities should review their arrangements for the co-ordination of services, both voluntary and statutory, for the under-fives, with a view to designating an official to be responsible for the co-ordination of these services.
>
> (DES 1981, p.76)

This was an important recommendation, as there is, as yet, no co-ordinated comprehensive system of under-five child care and educational provision in Britain. The importance of the issue for ethnic minorities is highlighted by information from the 1981 Census, which indicated that while ethnic minorities as a whole constitute about 4% of Britain's total population, ethnic minority children under five constitute nearly 7% of the total child population under five (Ballard 1983).

As with all the issues discussed so far, pre-school provision is a complex area fraught with problems and conflicting interests. It is, however, an area in which some practitioners are now making serious efforts to make more suitable provision for ethnic minority children. This chapter briefly reviews pre-school provision in general, and the models on which this provision is based. It then examines the pre-school requirements of minorities – particularly the requirements of working mothers for child-care – and notes the problems engendered by ethnocentric ideas of child-rearing. The chapter then looks at home and pre-school liaison and parent involvement in pre-schooling, at language difficulties, and at the crucial problem of initiating young children into 'two cultures' where the majority culture is regarded as 'superior'.

Pre-school provision
Pre-school provision is currently divisive and uncoordinated, with responsibility in the public sector being split between health, social and educational services, with provision also is offered by a variety of private and voluntary organisations. There are also, as Aplin and Pugh have pointed out, 'unreal distinctions made between care and education' (1983, p.9); and there is much social ambivalence about providing services for the under-fives, which has allowed for considerable political manipulation of the services, the children and their parents. Historically, there have been two types of provision for pre-school children: the day nursery – administered by health and welfare services, catering mainly for working-class children in urban areas, and stressing the health and welfare of the child – and the nursery school or class administered by the education authorities, stressing social and educational development and taking children from the age of three or four. 'Child-minding' was also officially recognised as a form of child-care provision from 1948, and in 1970 responsibility for nurseries and registered child-minding was transferred from the local authority health services to the social services. Arrangements for pre-school children continue to be a permissive, rather than a mandatory duty on local authorities. A Community Relations Commission report in 1975 noted that the social services tended to model their day-care services on theories of preventive social work – the assumption being that most 'normal' parents do not need such services, and that disadvantaged or handicapped children will tend to be the main clients of this form of care (CRC 1975, p.14). Such a model has not been an appropriate one for ethnic minority parents, as it has confused their 'normal' needs with those of a section of the population deemed to be inadequate.

There has been a steady increase in private and voluntary provision in both care and education. In 1962 a voluntary pre-school play-group movement began, largely as a middle-class initiative, which stressed the involvement of mothers and the educational development of children through play. There has also been some expansion of pre-school educational services, particularly in urban areas, where some schools have become the base for mother and toddler groups, toy libraries, parents' rooms and other developments. Many of these latter projects have been funded by the Urban Aid Programme, originally set up in 1968 to fund projects for ethnic minorities. Two separate professional groups are trained to care for under-fives: nursery nurses, certificated by the National Nursery Examination Board (NNEB), and nursery teachers, trained as educationists. Neither group has a history of encouraging parental involvement in under-five provision.

The Plowden recommendations (1967) were particularly influential in the area of nursery education, arguing that more urban nursery classes would help combat the effects of social and material disadvantage, and would help non-English speaking children. Tizard *et al.* (1976) in their critique of under-five provision, were able to record that by 1976 an extra 24,000 nursery school places had been made available via Urban Aid, and the Home Affairs Committee (1981, p.254) was also enthusiastic about the use of Urban Aid to increase educational provision for the under-fives. The proposed increases in pre-school educational provision at the beginning of the 1970s had encouraged the funding of a large-scale pre-school research study in Oxfordshire (Bruner 1980). However, by the time this project was complete and publications began to appear, and Bruner had pointed out the detrimental consequences for the younger generation if more pre-school provision were not made available, government was already cutting back on pre-school services.

During the 1970s, the provision of both day-care and education for under-fives became more inadequate as more parents, particularly single-parent families, sought such services. The 1971 Census demonstrated that one in three unsupported mothers worked, compared to one in five of the general population; and of these 55% worked over thirty hours and thus needed all-day care facilities (OPCS 1971). State provision for the children of working parents has always been inadequate. Allen (1979, p.139) wrote that, 'the position of working parents in the population as a whole has not been recognised by government, and many of the existing forms of provision do not begin to meet their needs'. The needs of working mothers for day-care, in particular, have been frustrated by ambiguous social attitudes. Ambivalence about provision of care for the under-fives has usually centred on a debate as to how far state provision should supersede or complement family care; whether mothers 'should' work; and whether the 'needs' of children, parents or employers should take precedence.

Political manipulation of the issue has been apparent in the way services have been provided when women's labour was required, and removed when this labour was no longer needed. Thus, the expansion of day-care services during the war, and its subsequent post-war run-down, has been well documented (Allen 1979; Summerfield 1982). However, the inadequacies of the services, combined with the increase in the number of two-parent working families and working single parents, has resulted in an increase in private day nurseries and child-minding. Despite research which suggests that two-thirds of all parents would like improved state facilities for under-fives (90% of parents of three to four year olds wanting day-care and educational facilities), only 40% are at present in some form of provision (see Bone 1977; Hughes *et al.* 1980, DES 1983). Of this 40%, more than half are in private or voluntary provision.

The National Child-Care Campaign, a pressure group dedicated to the creation of 'comprehensive, flexible, free, democratically controlled child-care facilities funded by the state'[1], has recently pointed out the extent to which even the existing inadequate services are being reduced. Fifty-two local authorities have reduced places in day nurseries over the past four years, 13 have cut expenditure on nursery education, and 49 have reduced grants to voluntary groups and registered child-minders (National Child-Care Campaign 1983). Thus, pre-school provision post-war has always been susceptible to changing views about the role of parents — particularly mothers — and to the changing requirements for female labour, and is an easy target for cuts in times of economic recession. The model on which much pre-school provision is based — that of services for disadvantaged people — militates against a comprehensive co-ordinated service used by all parents, and creates particular difficulties for minority parents, who need more and better day care and improved pre-school education.

Minority child-care requirements

A major requirement of minority parents over the past twenty-five years has been for adequate day-care provision while parents worked. Ethnic minority families, as the Community Relations Commission pointed out in 1975, are 'as a group, over-represented in the category of low income families, the mothers of such families are more likely to be at work and to work longer hours than other mothers' (CRC 1975, p.9). Mothers of West Indian origin are more likely to be working and to be single parent heads of households. Smith (1977) reported that in the mid-1970s, 75% of all West Indian women aged 16-54 years were working, compared to 55% of the general female population, and 47% of Asian women. He commented then that 'better facilities for the care of the children of these working mothers is needed' (p.66).

Phizaklea (1982) has remarked that, from the early 1960s, West Indian women took on a role of supplying cheap and flexible labour power in the economy, and a rapidly increasing female Asian labour force is joining them in this role. West Indian working women have experienced discrimination in the labour force and, being unable to find adequate child-care provision, have been particularly susceptible to punitive attitudes directed towards working mothers, and to stereotypes surrounding the use of child-minders. It was noted in Chapter Two that much of the 1960s literature about West Indian families was derogatory about differences in child-rearing and the role of the mother (for example, Fitzherbert 1967; Hood 1970); and many teachers came to hold stereotyped beliefs that the poorer educational performance on the part of some West Indian children could be traced to working mothers and child-minding. Literature which stressed the inadequacies of child-minding by untrained 'minders' (for example, Jackson and Jackson 1979) may unwittingly have contributed to these stereotypes. Minders themselves, even registered trained minders, have usually been regarded as a 'second-best' to day nurseries. The National Union of Teachers wrote in 1978:

> This union deplores the fact that child-minding services must be used in the absence of ordinary nursery school and day-care facilities . . . this particularly affects children of West Indian origin.
>
> (NUT 1978, p.11).

The numbers of all children left with minders are unknown. The Community Relations Commission estimated in 1975 that 150,000 children were probably in the care of minders (CRC 1975), and during the 1970s there was a sustained effort by local authorities to seek out, register and train child-minders. Leicester, for example, has been noted for pioneering alternative sources of day-care and has appointed full-time child minding supervisors (CRC 1975; Home Affairs Committee 1981). The National Children's Centre, a voluntary organisation, was set up in Huddersfield in 1975 to develop training for child-minders and support for working mothers. However, child-minding continues to be regarded as a less acceptable form of day-care, and Bryant *et al.* who studied minders as part of the Oxford pre-school project, recommended that no more minders should be registered, (Bryant *et al.* 1981).

The assumption that day nursery provision must always be superior to child-minding, particularly for non-white children, may be questionable. Ingham (1982), who studied 20 West Indian and 20 'white' children in a London nursery, suggested that the day nursery staff had difficulty in interacting with the West Indian children – particularly the boys. She concluded that if contact with adults is crucial to the development of cognitive and social skills, day nursery staff may be disadvantaging rather than helping young boys of West Indian origin.

Ethnocentric views of child-rearing

The quality of pre-school care and education provided for minority children has recently become as much a focus for attention as its quantity. The Commission for Racial Equality is currently producing a booklet on under-five provision, and a 'pack' for all practitioners and workers with the under-fives, aimed at combatting ethnocentric and racist beliefs and attitudes (Commission for Racial Equality 1983). A black working party attached to the National Child-Care Campaign is also particularly concerned about the quality of care for under-fives and the materials, books and toys, which are used with young children (see newsletter of black working party, National Child-Care Campaign 1983); and the National Association for Multiracial Education is also in the process of producing a policy statement on the under-fives, raising issues concerning both quantity and quality of care and education (NAME 1983).

The way in which all practitioners in pre-school care and education, whether they are professionally trained or voluntary workers, perceive and treat ethnic minority children depends very much on their own beliefs about what constitutes 'normal' child-rearing. It is currently the case that many theories about child-rearing which inform staff training, and 'commonsense' beliefs, are very ethnocentric, and are historically specific to Western industrial societies. The post-war 'maternal deprivation' hypothesis (Bowlby 1952) which in its vulgarised form was taken to support the belief that five years of care by a 'mother' was essential for normal child development, both provided a rationalisation for discouraging working mothers and led to the denigration of maternal behaviour in other cultures. Phizaklea has pointed out, for example, that in the West Indies, the woman's concept of the motherhood role includes the provision of financial support for the child (Phizaklea 1982, p.102). Theories stressing the need for women to be continuously with their pre-school children are of very recent origin, and are quite specific to richer industrial countries.

Theories stressing the importance of play and 'free expression' by children, popularised in the USA and Britain from the 1930s (see for example Isaacs 1946) are also culture-specific, and can lead to cultural misunderstandings. Barbara Tizard and her co-workers noted, in their most useful study of parental involvement in nursery and infant schools, that misunderstanding between teachers and minority parents could easily arise:

> Implicit in the teacher's approach to nursery education was the belief that a certain amount of dirtiness and disorder is desirable or at least acceptable in

children – but parents who put a high value on hard work, cleanliness, obedience and the acquisition of skills are not likely to warm to the sight of their children splashing in the water tray. (Tizard *et al.* 1981, p.63).

Likewise, the relatively recent Western assumption that young children should not be involved in adult 'work' can lead to denigration of minority cultural attributes and behaviour. Stereotypes denigrating the involvement of Chinese children in family businesses and of Asian girls in domestic tasks indicate an ethnocentric acceptance of 'non-work' by children; a by no means universally accepted assumption.

Optimistic beliefs in the relative innocence of young children about race and colour, stemming from assimilationist notions of the 1960s, have also affected the attitudes of staff in under-fives provision. The Commission for Racial Equality reported from a survey of multiracial day nurseries in 1977 that many staff though that 'colour differences were not significant to young children' (CRE 1977 p.17). However, there is now sufficient research on children's racial awareness (see Milner 1983), and a recognition that pre-school provision is a crucial area in which to begin to combat racial inequalities, for such beliefs to be discarded by pre-school staff.

There is some evidence that the trainers of staff for the under-fives are beginning to recognise these ethnocentric views of child-rearing. The National Nursery Examination Board has included, in their syllabus for nursery nurses, study of 'different cultural and sub-cultural patterns of family functioning' (National Nursery Examination Board 1983), and Chapter Three of this book has noted some of the attempts currently being made to permeate all teacher-training courses with multicultural and 'anti-racist' awareness, extending down to the pre-school level.

Parental pre-school involvement
The notion that parental involvement in the pre-school education of children is crucial both to the children's 'normal' development and to later success in schooling, has become widely accepted. Allied to this is the belief that if parents can themselves be 'educated' in appropriate parenting skills, their children's intellectual, social, emotional and physical development will be improved. These beliefs were central to the American and British compensatory education movements of the 1960s and early 1970s; urban 'disadvantaged' parents and ethnic minorities became the targets for professionals concerned to improve the quality of 'parenting'. Aplin and Pugh, in a discussion of the development of home-visiting, have pointed to the possible consequences of these beliefs. There has been an 'explosion' of professional expertise where 'tablets of wisdom are handed down by those who know, to those who need to know', and this may have undermined the confidence of many

parents in bringing up their own children (Aplin and Pugh 1983, p.8). Much home pre-school liaison has been based on the assumption that professionals can assist certain parents to be more aware of the 'right' way to care for and educate pre-school children: for example, the Home-Start Scheme in Leicester (Van der Eyken 1982), the Lothian Home-Visiting Scheme in Hampshire (Parker, 1982), and the Inner London Home-Visiting Scheme (Marsh and Scribbens 1982). However, assumptions that there are 'right' or appropriate ways of bringing up children can be both class-biased and ethnocentric; the priorities of minority parents, their views of child-rearing, their expectations about pre-school care and education, their understanding of parental involvement, may all be very different from those of white professionals and practitioners.

There is very little research examining the views of minority parents as to what kind of parental involvement in the pre-school care and education of their children they think is necessary and desirable. Even when parental views and cooperation are sought, professionals from different cultural and educational backgrounds may still work within ethnocentric models, or feel that professionals' expertise dictates that 'they know best'. One project which attempted to involve urban working class and minority mothers in the pre-school care and education of their children (a joint Open University and LEA project)[2] found difficulty in incorporating the suggestions, and reflecting the life-styles, of inner city parents and their children. One part of the project aimed at producing 'parenting materials'; but the booklets and stories produced by parents were felt to be inappropriate by the academics, while the parents felt that the materials produced by the professionals were not always useful or suitable. Yates wrote in her project report:

> The materials [produced by the professionals] were least appropriate for black groups – Asian and Afro-Caribbean. They neither reflected their life-styles, nor were written in a language they could understand . . . Some of the topics the Asian women found extremely embarrassing . . . neither did the materials in any way address people who, for instance, were single parents living in high-rise flats . . . Many of the illustrations reflected the ideal home similar to the dream home presented daily by the media (Yates 1982, p.1).

Yates felt, like Aplin and Pugh, that this kind of exercise, where professionals first sought the cooperation and involvement of parents, and then rejected their offerings as inappropriate, 'served to reinforce people's feelings of guilt and inadequacy, undermining their confidence as parents'.

Tizard and her co-workers, in their study of parental involvement in pre-school and nursery education, also found that minority parents' expectations and views about parental involvement differed greatly from the expectations and understandings of the staff. The 'cultural gap' between staff and Asian parents remained particularly wide.

There are, however, some positive efforts being made to understand the views and requirements of ethnic minority parents and to develop mutual understanding. Tizards' study included suggestions for the involvement of minority group parents in their children's pre-school education (Tizard *et al.* 1981, Chapter 14), and the National Child-Care Campaign's black working party encourages black parent groups to discuss their views and needs with pre-school staff. In Coventry, a community education project has set up an early learning project which sets out to 'train' mothers as leaders of mother and toddler groups, and to teach other mothers about modern nursery school materials. A number of the 'trained mothers' are from ethnic minority groups. Yates has also recorded the successful efforts made by the staff of a day-nursery to arrive at a working relationship with a group of black mothers who had initially been hostile to white views:

> The group was formed at the request of the nursery head, primarily because she wanted to encourage parental participation in her nursery. The children who attend the nursery are predominantly of Afro-Caribbean descent . . . most of the women are young, single mothers who live in either high-rise flats or maisonettes and some would identify themselves as fringe members of the Rastafari cult.

The nursery staff made positive efforts towards mutual understanding with the black mothers, inviting them to spend a day working side-by-side in the nursery, and discussing issues the mothers felt to be important for their children's future — including the 1981 British Nationality Bill and its possible effects on their children. Eventually, 'the relationship between the staff and parents grew into a caring partnership. This is reflected in the way that parents volunteer to help with activities and events [in the nursery], and the mothers openly discuss what they feel to be not only their children's but also their own learning difficulties with the staff' (Yates 1982, p.11).

Language issues

A major issue in pre-school provision for ethnic minority children is that of language, and there is a variety of debates — about the teaching of English as a second language, the retention of mother-tongue, the problems of bilingualism and bidialectalism — which all affect the education of pre-school children. The presence of children whose first language is not English, and particularly 'non-English speakers', has always been regarded as problematic by infant and nursery school teachers. There is general agreement that if a young child habitually speaks a language at home different from that used in school, he or she will be at a disadvantage educationally (see Derrick 1977; Davies 1982). Minority parents have always expected schools to teach their children English. Tizard noted in her study of nursery and infant schools that minority parents are very concerned that their children should learn English (Tizard 1981). However, while teaching English as a second language to school pupils has usually been a priority there has been less stress on structured language teaching at the pre-school level. Derrick has noted that from the 1960s many teachers have believed that 'English could brush-off on the reasonably young immigrant child by virtue of his being in an English-speaking school' (Derrick 1977, p.9), and that children could 'pick up' English. This belief may still be quite common. Tizard reported that nursery teachers in her study seemed relatively unconcerned about the linguistic needs of the (largely Asian) children in her study schools, and that 'if they had put more emphasis on ESL, kept records of children's progress, discussed these with parents, and suggested ways in which parents could help, the parents would have been better pleased' (Tizard *et al.* 1981, p.62). The Bullock report in 1975 had also noted that in infant and nursery classes, teachers showed reluctance to do any 'formal' language work, on the grounds that 'they would learn to speak English anyway' (Bullock 1975, p.292).

West Indian parents are also anxious that their children should become fluent in standard English as early as possible. As the chapter on supplementary schools indicated, in these schools the emphasis is firmly on standard English, and Mungo, a black teacher, in a review of the use of dialects in schools, concluded that 'internationally accepted English' was what black children needed to acquire at an early age (Mungo 1979).

There is now more recognition that young West Indian children who speak dialect rather than standard English at home may have considerable problems in an educational setting. Sutcliffe (1978, 1982) and Edwards (1979) have concluded that the children do not easily become bidialectal, and that dialect 'interference' can affect educational performance at an early age. In addition, if nursery staff or teachers regard dialect as 'inferior' speech, the motivation of young West Indian children to acquire standard English may be affected. While sociolinguistic research concerning the problems young children experience in becoming bidialectal or bilingual is now at a sophisticated level (see Simoes 1976; Edwards 1983), there is little evidence that nursery or infant school teachers are aware of the debates and problems, and are prepared, during their training, to help minority children whose first language is not standard English.

The Bullock report in 1975 was probably influential in persuading teachers that minorities had a right to retain their cultural and linguistic identity in a plural society, and that, 'No child should be expected to cast off the language and culture of home as he crosses the school threshold' (Bullock 1975); by 1982 the National Union of Teachers had published a booklet on mother-tongue teaching emphasising that 'to value the language and culture is to value the child' (NUT 1982).

The use of 'mother-tongue' as a transitional medium through which children gradually acquire the majority language has been researched and discussed in other countries (see Hornby 1977), and in Britain several research projects are studying the educational implications of teaching in both mother tongue and English. A project at Bradford, the MOTET project (see Chapman 1980) is studying the effects of teaching Punjabi-speaking children partly in Punjabi during their first year at school; and the results appear to indicate that the children's educational performance is better than a control group taught only through the medium of English. Lewis, in 1970, had pointed out that early exposure to conflicting languages and cultures could lead to severe difficulties for pre-school children; and Derrick, in her 1977 book, developed this point to suggest that nursery staff should always take account of the mother tongue and culture of minority group children. For example, if possible, mother tongue speakers should be employed in nurseries, to offer the children a sense of continuity between home and nursery (Derrick 1977, p.51).

However, although some teachers are now becoming more knowledgeable about, and sympathetic to, the language and dialect problems of pre-school minority children, it is perhaps not surprising that many still remain ambivalent about the encouragement of minority languages. Teachers may well be very conscious of the problems of introducing young children to two languages and two cultures simultaneously, but lacking advice and guidance may well decide, as Tizard's teachers had decided, to ignore the issue. This situation may be in the process of changing – albeit slowly. A recent survey by Craft and Atkins (1973) indicated that approximately half of all initial teacher training institutions now make some mention of issues relating to linguistic diversity.

Two cultures

Debates about the pre-school care and education of minority children are often conducted on a cultural level; the children are deemed to have problems because they are being introduced to two cultures simultaneously. It is undoubtedly true that the children who, though born in Britain, have to acquire two or more languages and accommodate to two or more sets of cultural values, face major problems not encountered by indigenous children. These problems are exacerbated by a situation in which the cultures and languages of non-white minorities are not accorded the same status and respect as that offered to 'European' cultures. Pre-school staff may well be affected by a social climate in which the customs and behaviour of minorities are misunderstood, regarded as less important, or even derided.

In addition, the young children of minority parents face socio-political problems in British society. Because of differences in race, colour, culture and language, minority children will grow up with a different structural relationship to the society than will majority children. In particular, the socio-political debate as to what the relationship of the next generation of non-white ethnic minority children will be to the society is still undecided.

Practitioners in all areas of minority pre-school care and education have not only, therefore, to be aware of problems engendered by cultural and linguistic differences, and by the ethnocentrism and racism of the wider society of which they are a part; they must also be aware of political debates about the future relationship between minorities and the majority society in Britain. Pre-school provision is not an unimportant area where these issues can be comfortably ignored, it is a crucial one where the problems should be openly debated.

Summary

This chapter has examined some of the issues concerning pre-school provision for ethnic minority children. The Rampton Committee (DES 1981) had emphasised the importance of this area by placing recommendations concerning pre-school first in their list of suggestions for the improved education of minority children. The chapter briefly explored the development of pre-school education in Britain as a context for understanding provision for minority children, and noted that although there is a rising demand for both 'care' and education, cutbacks are already operating. The particular requirements of minority parents – particularly of West Indian parents, for child-care while parents work – have not been met, and stereotypes connected with child-minding have made life more difficult for West Indian parents. The assumption that day nurseries are always superior to other forms of care, for minority children, may be questionable. Ethnocentric views of child-rearing and 'normal' child development were noted, as these views affect the attitudes of pre-school staff towards minority parents and their children.

Parental involvement in pre-school education, and the inappropriate models of 'inadequate' parents on which much of this involvement is based, was discussed. Efforts to involve minority parents may founder on cultural and class bias, and professionals may decide that, after all, 'they know best'. Language problems in pre-school education were briefly raised, and deeper issues concerning bringing up children in 'two cultures' and in a hostile majority society, were touched upon.

Notes

1. The National Child-Care Campaign is a voluntary pressure group with the aim of building 'a mass national child care campaign around the demand for comprehensive, flexible, free, democratically controlled child care facilities funded by the state, thus recognising that child-care provision is necessary to meet the needs of children and parents.' (National Child-Care Campaign, 17 Victoria Park Square, London, publicity leaflet).

2. Van Leer/Open University project on parenting materials, 1979-82. Areas used for research were Birmingham, Coventry, Liverpool and the Western Isles of Scotland.

8 Home-School Co-operation

There are no easy solutions to the problems and tensions arising between homes and schools in a multicultural society. Improved parent-teacher contact, better home-school liaison, more home-school co-operation – these can easily become rhetorical objectives, seemingly easy to implement but in fact very difficult to put into practice. It is now easier, with hindsight, to see that some of the conflicts between minority homes and schools over the past twenty-five years were bound to arise. During that time, minority parents have been struggling to understand an unfamiliar education system, of which they had high expectations and which appeared to promise a good deal, but which did not necessarily honour its promises. Schools and teachers, with little information or preparation, have struggled to accommodate minority children in a system designed for a white majority, and to understand the views of minority parents. Lack of knowledge on both sides, mismatches of expectations, and clashes of values, rather than mutual understanding, have tended to characterise minority home-school contacts. However, if home-school problems are to be solved and tensions minimised in the future, ethnic minority parents must feel they are getting a fair deal from the education system, and teachers must feel that minority parents are working with them and supporting them.

This final chapter draws together some of the major problem areas and suggests some policies for improved practice.

Minority parents and disadvantage
Although it was noted in Chapter One that, historically, there has been no general acceptance that parents – particularly manual working-class parents – should be involved in the state education of their children to any great extent, major efforts to change this situation have been made over the past fifteen years. Parental 'rights' now have more legal backing, parents are slowly becoming more involved in educational decision-making, the mechanisms of improved home-school contact are under discussion, and more professionalisation of the area is under way. Debates have been based on the assumption that co-operation between

parents and teachers is educationally desirable, and that children's school performance and attainment improves when home and school act in partnership.

However, in these debates the place of minority parents has seldom been discussed or considered. In the literature on home-school relations minority homes are invisible, are conceptualised as 'problems', or are subsumed under a wider group – that of the 'disadvantaged'. It has been a recurring theme of this book that the stereotype of the 'disadvantaged' parent, who is in need of organisation by professionals and whose children are in need of 'compensation' for their background, is inappropriate when applied to minority communities. Indeed, the model adds further stigmatisation to groups already at a disadvantage in society. Teachers who view minority parents and pupils as disadvantaged are, as we saw in Chapter Three, more likely to stress material and environmental factors, rather than disadvantages connected with racial discrimination.

Much home-school liaison is at the moment based on the model of disadvantage, and professionals, as noted in Chapters Six and Seven, may still feel that their expertise guarantees that 'they know best', a position which precludes really listening to parents' views and opinions. Models of disadvantage may also be ethnocentric, and professionals from white middle-class backgrounds may denigrate minority child-rearing patterns and parental behaviour. Teachers working within the disadvantage model may come to view their work more in a social-pastoral care context than an examination-oriented or skill-oriented one: schools for the disadvantaged are not places where high academic achievement is expected. Teachers' views may thus clash with the expectations of minority parents, who do expect their children to achieve examination passes or acquire skills that will be vocationally useful.

All in all, the simple categorisation of ethnic minority parents as 'disadvantaged' may have actually contributed to the crisis of confidence and the 'gulf in trust and understanding' (DES 1981) between minority homes and schools. Despite the undoubted social and material disadvantages to be found in urban areas, minority parents do *not* consider themselves to be part of a disadvantaged group, forming, as Myrdal once wrote of the American poor, an 'inert and despairing social residue' (Myrdal 1964)[1]. Minority parents and communities are increasingly articulating their own needs, acting together to solve their problems, and organising in their own interests. The development of supplementary education is a good example of this process in the educational field.

Equality of opportunity

A second theme of this book has been that there is a mismatch of expectations between schools and minority parents. Migrant parents have always been eager for their children to take advantage of an education system which appeared to offer social and economic rewards; and minority parents have become increasingly anxious that schools did not seem able to equip their children with the required qualifications and skills to compete 'equally' with white children. This anxiety has been particularly acute for West Indian parents. It is not surprising that the issue of school achievement has come to dominate home-school relations in West Indian communities. However, it was noted in Chapter Four that the basis of this mismatch of expectations may lie more in the structure and functions of the education system than in any parental failure or teacher obtuseness. Although the structure of the state system changed with moves to comprehensivisation, equality of opportunity to be selected for an academic education did not increase for the children of manual working-class parentage. Inner-city schools – those primarily attended by manual working-class children and minority children, have seldom been able to offer opportunities equal even to those of suburban comprehensive schools. The function of these schools has never been to provide the traditional 'grammar-school' education many minority parents expected. However, it has been difficult to explain this to the parents, and home and school have often resorted to a process of 'blaming' each other. Since it has never been part of the English education system to explain too clearly to parents why promises of 'equal opportunity' are not possible in practice, tensions between minority homes and schools have been further exacerbated. It is ironic that at a time when the traditional academic curriculum is increasingly being questioned as a suitable preparation for all children in the technological society of the future, minority parents, not being informed or drawn into discussions of change, are becoming increasingly committed to it.

Cultural diversity

If the structure and functions of the education system work against the expectations of minority parents and cause problems, the value-base of the system may also be an inbuilt source of tension. The recognition and implementation of cultural diversity may be in the interests of social and racial justice, and the retention of different cultural traditions and heritage an essential part of a plural society; but if a minority group cultural heritage incorporates values that are at odds with the values of the education system, problems may well be insoluble. It was noted in Chapter Four that the cultural content of the English education system may be distinctly at odds with Islamic values. For example, the long-term resistance of many schools and teachers to the desires of Muslim parents for a different education for girls, may well have been based on a value developing over the past hundred and fifty years, that girls in Britain should have equal opportunities in the same, rather than in separate spheres of life, as boys. It will never be an easy task to reconcile the values inherent in Islamic education with the values of the British education system. A wider question, addressed by Craft in 1982, is how far the education system can educate for diversity, without putting social cohesion in the whole society at risk:

> Cultural pluralism sets the sternest tests for our political ideals, in presenting a tension between education for diversity and education for consensus.
>
> (Craft 1982, p.13)

If minority parents do want their children to be offered equal opportunities in British schools, there may be limits to the kind of cultural diversity which schools, on the basis of their own values, can encourage. This is a problem which schools, teachers and parents will have to discuss seriously, in the future, and try to arrive at some kind of compromise. The discussions with minority parents described in Chapter Four, in 'Northern School', indicate that this kind of communication is possible. The starting point for such discussions, however, should be that minority cultural values and traditions have equal status and are not inferior to those of the majority society.

Improved practice

It has been acknowledged throughout the book that there has been some progress in furthering general home-school links, particularly during the past fifteen years. To improved 'old-style' links (parent-teacher meetings, written school communication with homes, more parent-teacher associations, more professional educational liaison, and the beginnings of some pre-school parental involvement) have been added 'new-style' links — some parental participation in educational decision-making via governing bodies and elected committees, and consultation between the 'community' and LEAs. Some of these improved practices have benefited minority communities, and indeed some LEAs with large numbers of minority parents have been in the forefront of such developments. It remains an important question, however, as to how far policies to improve home-school relations should be specifically aimed at minority parents, and how far at all parents.

One particular policy, adopted on a national scale for all parents, could be of particular benefit to minority parents. This is the 'school and family concordat' proposed by MacBeth (1983) in the conclusions to his report on school-family relations in the countries of the European Community. MacBeth has pointed out that despite some improved home-school liaison, educational *partnership* between home and school has never really emerged. Exhortation by government committees and initiatives on the part of *some* LEAs and schools have produced patchy developments, and there are still no recognisable national policies for furthering home-school partnership. MacBeth has suggested a formalised contract between homes and schools:

> A framework of contractual obligations for both teachers and parents – more specific than those expressed in general laws at the moment.
>
> (MacBeth 1983, p.231)

Parents would sign a 'parents' contract' when their child enters school, by which they would undertake to co-operate with the school in specific ways. The school and teachers would have contractual liaison obligations to the parents. In this way, a friendly but professional relationship could be established at the start of the child's education. While MacBeth has discussed the possible problems of such a 'concordat' in some detail, he has particularly stressed that such a contract would require knowledge and understanding on both sides, and this would be of particular value for minority home-school relations. If schools had a contractual obligation to co-operate with minority homes, and to explain the educational process, teaching methods, curriculum and examinations, and the limits and possibilities of schooling, minority parents would be less likely to misunderstand and 'blame' teachers and more likely to work *with* schools. Similarly, if parents had obligations to give active support to their children's education, to support school rules and regulations, and to learn about school processes, teachers might feel they had the support of knowledgeable parents, rather than the antagonism of uninformed ones. MacBeth has also stressed that home-school liaison is primarily about education. It is not about parents being diverted into fund-raising and social activities for schools, and it is also *not* about social work with 'disadvantaged' parents. A school-parent concordat might set the present uneasy relationship between minority homes and schools on a more professional basis, that would enhance the professional status and responsibility of teachers, and begin to make minority parents see themselves as more knowledgeable partners supporting the education of their children.

A second policy to further home-school links could be the setting up of more positive parental organisations among minority communities, rather than the sometimes negatively-oriented parents' groups who, understandably, have come together in the past to share anxieties about their children's education. Schools could then have a duty to consult and liaise with such organisations. Again, looking to the European Community, models of positive parental organisations have already been provided. A recent public statement by representatives from 40 parents' organisations in the EEC put forward a list of objectives for such organisations. They were:

- to make parents aware of their role (rights and duties) in regard to schools

- to inform parents about the school education of their children *and to inform schools about parental expectations*

- to develop an active partnership within the education community, and to ensure that parents are represented and participate at all levels of the education system

- to assist parents to acquire the skills their role demands

- to seek to be consulted *and to participate at all levels* in the decision-making processes which affect their children

- to promote the development of the educational services

(EEC 1983)

Dialogue promoted by such positively-oriented parental organisations could go far to remove current tensions and misunderstandings between minority homes and schools.

A third policy, perhaps specifically aimed at minority homes, should be concerned with the pre-school level. The needs of minority working parents for adequate, non-stigmatised child care by properly trained staff, who do not view child-rearing from ethnocentric perspectives, have been commented on in Chapter Seven. But the pre-school education of minority children should perhaps be a target for national policy. The opportunity for all minority children to attend a nursery school or class, taught by staff who are aware of the problems engendered by linguistic, cultural and racial differences, and who have been specially trained to bridge the gap between minority homes and schools, should be a priority. If minority parents' expectations are to be met and their co-operation secured, a proper *education* for their children must begin before the age of compulsory schooling.

Improved relationships and practices between minority homes and schools will depend on improved training and assistance for teachers. The area of home-school relationships should now be taken much more seriously by senior staff. MacBeth has remarked that 'the commitment of school management to home-school liaison is essential. If leadership is half-hearted, cynical or hostile, the worthiest efforts of those in the school community are bound to be damaged.' (MacBeth 1983, p.243). Now that there is more general acceptance that in the future, senior staff in schools will need management training, relationships with homes and parents can become an essential part of such training courses. Effective home-school liaison, and positive partnership between teachers and parents, should become a professional goal of senior school management and not an optional extra to be left to chance.

Whatever new policies may be adopted, it is certain that offering more of the palliatives often substituted in the past for 'home-school contacts' — repeating recommendations and exhortations to action, while at the same time taking a cynical or dismissive attitude towards homes and parents — will not solve the crisis of confidence between minority homes and schools. The issue at stake is the ability of schools to educate minority pupils in accordance with principles of social and racial justice — to offer equal opportunities and to respect racial and cultural differences and diversity — and this demands new and more radical home-school policies than those previously available. Relationships between homes and schools are not a minor issue, they are crucial to the success of a multicultural society.

Notes
1. For further discussion of definitions of the disadvantaged, see Rex and Tomlinson 1979, particularly note to Chapter One.

Select Bibliography

AHMED, S.(1981), 'Asian Girls and Culture Conflict', in Cheetham, J. (Ed.), *Social and Community Work in a Multi-Racial Society*, Harper and Row/Open University Press.

ALL FAITHS FOR ONE RACE (AFFOR) (1982), *Talking Chalk: Black Pupils, Parents and Teachers Speak about Education*, Handsworth, Birmingham.

ALLEN, S. (1979), 'Pre-School Children. Ethnic Minorities in Britain', *New Community*, Vol. 7, No. 2., pp.135-42.

ALLEN, S. (1983), 'Confusing Categories and Neglecting Contradictions', in CASHMORE, E. and TROYNA, B., (Eds.), *Black Youth in Crisis*, Allen and Unwin.

ALTARF (All London Teachers against Racism and Facism) (1980), *Teaching and Racism. An ALTARF Discussion Document*, Centre for Urban Educational Studies.

ANWAR, M. (1979), *The Myth of Return*, Heinemann Educational Books.

APLIN, G. and PUGH, G. (1983), *Perspectives on Pre-School Visiting*, National Children's Bureau and Community Education Development Centre.

AULD REPORT (1976), *The William Tyndale Junior and Infant School* (Report of a public enquiry conducted by Mr. Robin Auld Q.C. into the teaching, organisation and management of the William Tyndale School), Inner London Education Authority.

AVON NATIONAL UNION OF TEACHERS (1980), *After the Fire. A Report on Education in St. Pauls, Bristol*, National Union of Teachers, Bristol.

BACON, J.M.D. (1978), *Public Accountability and the Schooling System*, Harper and Row.

BAGLEY, C. (1976), 'Behavioural Deviance in Ethnic Minority Children. A Review of Published Studies', *New Community*, Vol. 5, No. 3, pp.230-8.

BAGLEY, C., BART, M., WONG, J. (1979), 'Antecedents of Scholastic Success in West Indian Ten-Year-Olds in London', in VERMA, G.K., and BAGLEY, C., (Eds.), *Race, Education and Identity*, Macmillan.

BALLARD, C. (1979), 'Conflict, Continuity and Change. Second Generation South Asians', in KAHN, V.S. (Ed.), *Minority Families in Britain. Support and Stress*, Tavistock.

BALLARD, R. (1983), 'Race and the Census. What an "Ethnic Question", would show', *New Society*, 12.5.83, pp.212-14.

BALLARD, R. and BALLARD, C. (1977), 'The Sikhs. The Development of South Asian Settlement in Britain', in WATSON, J. (Ed.), *Between Two Cultures*, Oxford, Blackwell.

BANKS, J. (1981), *Multi-Ethnic Education. Theory and Practice*, Boston, Allyn and Bacon.

BARON, G. and HOWELL, D.A. (1974), *The Government and Management of Schools*, Athlone Press.

BASTIANI, J. (Ed.), (1978), *Written Communication between Home and School*, Institute of Education, University of Nottingham.

BASU, A. (1978), 'Policy and Conflict in India. The Reality and Perception of Education', in ALTBACH, P.G. and KELLY, G. (Eds.), *Education and Colonialism*, Longman, New York.

BAYLISS, S. (1982), 'Plain Speaking – or Status Quo', *Times Educational Supplement*, 15.10.82, p.23.

BAYLISS, S. (1983), 'L.E.A. gives Bigger Say to Parents', *Times Educational Supplement*, 20.5.83.

BEETHAM, D. (1967), *Immigrant School Leavers and the Youth Employment Service in Birmingham*, I.R.R. Special Series.

BENINGTON, J. (1977), 'The Flaw in the Pluralist Heaven', in RAYNOR, J. and HARRIS, E. (Eds.), *The City Experience*, Ward Lock/Open University Press.

BENNETT, S.N. (1979), 'Recent Research on Teaching – a Dream, a Belief, a Model', in BENNETT, S.N. and MCNAMARA, D. (Eds.), *Focus on Teaching*, Longman.

BENNETT, S.N. and MCNAMARA, D. (1979), *Focus on Teaching*, Longman.

BERKSHIRE DEPARTMENT OF EDUCATION (1982), *Education for Equality. A Paper for Discussion in Berkshire*, Advisory Committee on Multicultural Education, Berkshire.

BERNSTEIN, B. (1973), *Class, Codes and Control*, Routledge.

BHATTI, F.M. (1978), 'Young Pakistanis in Britain. Educational Needs and Problems', *New Community*, Vol. 6, No. 3.

BIDWELL, S. (1978), 'The Turban Victory', Southall, London, Sri Guru Singh Sabha.

BLACK ARROW SUPPLEMENTARY SCHOOL (1982) *Prospectus*, Wolverhampton.

BONE, M. (1977), *Pre-School Children and the Need for Day Care*, HMSO.

BOWLBY, J. (1952), *Maternal Care and Mental Health*, World Health Organisation, Geneva.

BRADFORD CITY COUNCIL (1982), *Education for a Multicultural Society. Provision for Pupils of Ethnic Minorities in Schools*, Bradford.

BRAH, A. (1978), 'Age, Race and Power. The Case of South Asian Youths in Britain' in DAY, M. and MARSLAND, D. (Eds.), *Black Kids, White Kids – What Hope*, National Youth Bureau, Leicester.

BRASS, T. (1983), 'Demographic Trends' (unpublished paper), Institute of Tropical Medicine, University of London.

BRITISH NATIONALITY ACT (1981), HMSO.

BRITTAN, E. (1976a), 'Multiracial Education. Teacher Opinion on Aspects of School Life. I. Changes in Curriculum and School Organisation', *Educational Research*, Vol. 18, No. 2.

BROADY, M. (1955), 'The Social Adjustment of Chinese Immigrants in Britain', *Sociological Review*, pp.65-75.

BRYANT, B., HARRIS, M., NEWTON, D. (1981), *Children and Minders*, Grant McIntyre.

BULLOCK, SIR A. (1975), *A Language for Life*, Report of a Committee of Enquiry, HMSO.

BRUNER, J. (1980), *Under-Fives in Britain*, Grant McIntyre.

CARBY, H. (1983), 'Schooling in Babylon', in CENTRE FOR CONTEMPORARY CULTURAL STUDIES (Ed.), *The Empire Strikes Back*, Hutchinson.

CARRINGTON, B. (1983), 'Sport as a side-track', in BARTON, L. and WALKER, S. (Eds.), *Race, Class and Education*, Bedenham, Croom Helm.

CASHMORE, E. (1979), *Rastaman*, Routledge.

CHAPMAN, L. (1980), 'An Experiment in Mother-Tongue Teaching', *Trends in Education*, No. 5, Department of Education and Science.

CHERRINGTON, D. and GILES, R. (1981), 'Present Provision in Initial Teacher Training' in CRAFT, M. (Ed.), *Teaching in a Multicultural Society. The Task for Teacher Education*, Brighton, Falmer Press.

CHEVANNES, M. (1979), 'The Black Arrow Supplementary School Project', *The Social Science Teacher*, Vol. 8, No. 4.

CHEVANNES, M. (1982), interview on 'Ebony', BBC TV, 17.11.82.

CITY OF COVENTRY (1976), *Position Statement on Race Relations*, Coventry.

CITY OF COVENTRY (1983), *Comprehensive Education for Life. A Consultative Document*, Coventry.

CLARK, N. (1982), 'Datchwyng Saturday School', in OHRI, A., MANNING, B., and CURNO. P. (Eds.), *Community Work and Racism,* Routledge.

CNAA (1982), *Agenda for Multicultural Education*, (unpublished discussion paper), Council for National Academic Awards.

COARD, B. (1972), *How the West Indian Child is made ESN in the British School System*, New Beacon Books.

COHEN, L. and MANION, L. (1983), *Multicultural Classrooms,* Beckenham, Croom Helm.

COMMISSION FOR RACIAL EQUALITY (1977), *Caring for Under-Fives in a Multi-racial Society*, CRE.

COMMISSION FOR RACIAL EQUALITY (1978), *Schools and Ethnic Minorities*, CRE.

COMMISSION FOR RACIAL EQUALITY (1983), *Ethnic Minority Children Under Five*, Working Group on Under-Fives, CRE.

COMMUNITY RELATIONS COMMISSION (1975), *Who Minds? A Study of Mothers and Child-Minding in Ethnic Minority Communities*, CRC.

CRAFT, M. (Ed.), (1970), *Family, Class and Education*, Longman.

CRAFT, M. (Ed.), (1981), *Teaching in a Multicultural Society: The Task for Teacher Education,* Brighton, Falmer Press.

CRAFT, M. (1982), *Education for Diversity. The Challenge of Cultural Pluralism*, (Inaugural Lecture), University of Nottingham, Nottingham.

CRAFT, M. and ATKINS, M. (1983), *Training Teachers of Ethnic Minority Community Languages*, A Report for the Swann Committee, University of Nottingham School of Education, Nottingham.

CRONIN, A. (1982), *Black Supplementary Schools* (unpub. paper), Department of Sociology, Polytechnic of North London.

CROSS, M. (1978), 'West Indians and the Problem of Metropolitan Majority', in *Black Kids, White Kids — What Hope*, DAVY, M. and MARSLAND, D. (Eds.). National Youth Bureau, Leicester.

CYSTER, R. and CLIFT, P. (1980), 'Parental Involvement in Primary Schools. The NFER Survey', in CRAFT, M. RAYNOR, J. and COHEN, L. (Eds.), *Linking Home and School* (3rd edition), Harper and Row.

DAHYA, B. (1974), 'The Nature of Pakistani Ethnicity in Industrial Cities in Britain', in COHEN, A. (Ed.), *Urban Ethnicity*, Tavistock.

DAVIES, A. (1982), *Language and Learning in Home and School*, Heinemann Educational Books.

DAVEY, A.G. and NORBURN, M.V. (1980), 'Ethnic Awareness and Ethnic Differentiation Amongst Primary School Children', *New Community*, Vol. 8, No. 1-2, pp.51-60.

DEPARTMENT OF EDUCATION AND SCIENCE (1974), *Educational Disadvantage and The Needs of Immigrants*, Cmnd. 5720, HMSO.

DEPARTMENT OF EDUCATION AND SCIENCE (1977), *Education in Schools. A Consultative Document*, HMSO.

DEPARTMENT OF EDUCATION AND SCIENCE (1981a) *West Indian Children in our Schools*, A Report of the Committee of Enquiry into the Education of Children from Ethnic Minority Groups (the 'Rampton Report'), HMSO.

DEPARTMENT OF EDUCATION AND SCIENCE (1981b), *Directive of the Council of the European Community on the Education of the Children of Migrant Workers*, Circular No. 5/81, DES.

DEPARTMENT OF EDUCATION AND SCIENCE (1982), *The New Teacher in School. HMI Discussion Document*, HMSO.

DEPARTMENT OF EDUCATION AND SCIENCE (1983), *Pupils Under Five in Each Local Education Authority in England*, 1982 Statistical Bulletin 8/83, DES.

DERRICK, J. (1968), 'School — the Meeting Point', in OAKLEY, R. (Ed.), *New Backgrounds*, OUP for IRR.

DERRICK, J. (1977), *Language Needs of Minority Group Children*, Slough, NFER.

DICKENSON, P. (1982), 'Facts and Figures — Some Myths' in TIERNEY, J. (Ed.), *Race, Migration and Schooling*, Holt, Rinehart and Winston.

DOSANJH, J.S. (1969), 'Punjabi Immigrant Children — Their Social and Educational Problems in Adjustment', *Education Paper No. 10*, University of Nottingham, Nottingham.

DOUGLAS, J.W.B. (1964), *The Home and the School*, MacGibbon and Kee.

DRIVER, G. (1977), 'Cultural Competence, Social Power and School Achievement. West Indian Secondary School Pupils in the Midlands', *New Community*, Vol. 5, No. 4.

DUMMETT, A. with MARTIN, I. (1982), *British Nationality*, Report by the Action Group on Immigration and Nationality, National Council for Civil Liberties.

EDMONDS, R. (1979), 'Effective Schools for the Urban Poor', *Educational Leadership*, October, pp.15-24.

EDUCATION ACT (1944), HMSO.

EDUCATION ACT (1980), HMSO.

EDWARDS, V.K. (1979), *The West Indian Language Issue in British Schools*, Routledge.

EGGLESTON, S.J. (1981), 'Present Provision in In-Service Training' in CRAFT, M. (Ed.), *Teaching in a Multicultural Society: The Task for Teacher Education*, Brighton, Falmer Press.

EGGLESTON, J. (1983), 'Ethnic Naïvety', *Times Educational Supplement*, 11.3.83.

ELLIS, J. (1978), *West African Families in Britain*, Routledge.

EUROPEAN ECONOMIC COMMUNITY (EEC) (1983), *Public Statement by Representatives of 40 Parent Organisations*, Luxembourg.

FINCH, J., FRY, P. and ANDERSON, P. (1980), *Report on the Home-School Project*, unpublished Report for Preston and Western Lancashire Council for Community Relations, Preston.

FINCH, J. (1984), *Education as Social Policy*, Longman.

FITZHERBERT, K. (1967), *West Indian Children in London*, Bell.

FLETCHER, C. and THOMPSON, N. (1980), *Issues in Community Education*, Brighton, Falmer Press.

FONER, N. (1979), *Jamaica Farewell*, Routledge.

FOWLER, R., LITTLEWOOD, B., and MADIGAN, R. (1977), 'Immigrant School Leavers and the Search for Work', *Sociology*, Vol. 11, No. 1.

FRANCIS, M. (1979), 'Disruptive Units – Labelling a New Generation', *New Approaches in Multiracial Education*, vol. 8, No. 1.

GARVEY, A. and JACKSON, B. (1975), *Chinese Children*, Cambridge, National Education Development Trust.

GAUTRY, R. (1937), *Lux Mihi Laus – School Board Memories*, Link House.

GHUMAN, P.A.S. (1980a), 'Punjabi Parents and English Education', *Educational Research*, Vol. 22, No. 2, pp.121-30.

GHUMAN, P. A. S. (1980b), 'Bhattra Sikhs in Cardiff. Family and Kinship Organisation', *New Community*, Vol. 8, No. 3 pp. 309-16.

GHUMAN, P.A.S. and GALLOP, R. (1981), 'Educational Attitudes of Bengali Families in Cardiff', *Journal of Multicultural and Multilingual Developement*, Vol. 2, No. 2.

GIBBES, N. (1980), *West Indian Teachers Speak Out*, Lewisham CRC and the Caribbean Teachers Association.

GILES, R. (1977), *The West Indian Experience in British Schools*, Heinemann.

GOACHER, B., WEINDLING, R., DE'KOCK, U. (1983), *School Reports. An Evaluation of Policy and Practice in the Secondary School*, Slough, NFER.

GOODY, E. and GROOTHUES, C.M. (1979), 'West African Couples in London' in KHAN, V.S. (Ed.), *Minority Families in Britain*, Tavistock.

GRACE, G. (1978), *Education, Ideology and Social Control*, Routledge.

GREEN, P.A. (1972), 'Attitudes of Teachers of West Indian Immigrant Groups' (unpublished M.Phil. Thesis) University of Nottingham.

GREEN, P.A. (1982), 'Teachers' Influence on the Self-Concept of Pupils of Different Ethnic Origins' (unpub. Ph.D. Thesis), University of Durham.

GROSS, M. (1982), Letter to *Times Educational Supplement*, 10.12.82.

BERLINER, W. (1982), 'Labour Reformer Upsets Teachers', *The Guardian*, 20 Dec. 1982, p.3.

GUPTA, P. (1977), 'Educational and Vocational Aspirations of Asian Immigrants and English School-Leavers', *British Journal of Sociology*, Vol. 28, No. 2, pp.185-98.

HALL, S. (1967), *The New Englanders*, Community Relations Commission.

HALSEY, A.H. (1972), *Educational Priority. EPA Problems and Policies*, Vol. 1, HMSO.

HALSEY, A.H., HEATH, A.F. and RIDGE, J.M. (1980), *Origins and Destinations — Family, Class and Education in Modern Britain*, Oxford, Clarendon Press.

HARGREAVES, D.H. (1983), *The Challenge for the Comprehensive School: Culture, Curriculum and Community*, Routledge

Hansard, Vol. 18, No. 58, Feb. 16th, House of Commons, London.

HARRIS, R. (1980), 'Parent-Teacher Contact. A Case Study', in CRAFT, M., RAYNOR, J., and COHEN, L. (Eds.), *Linking Home and School* (3rd edition), Harper and Row.

HASHMI, F. (1966), *The Pakistani Family in Britain*, Community Relations Commission.

HELWIG, A. W. (1979), *Sikhs in England. The Development of a Migrant Community*, Oxford, OUP.

HEWISON, J. and TIZARD, J. (1980), 'Parental Involvement and Reading Attainment', *British Journal of Educational Psychology*, Vol. 50, pp.209-15.

HIRO, D. (1967), *The Indian Family in Britain*, Community Relations Commission.

HOME AFFAIRS COMMITTEE (1981), *Racial Disadvantage*, 5th Report, HMSO.

HONEYFORD, R. (1982), 'Multi-Racial Myths', *Times Educational Supplement*, 19.11.82.

HOOD, C., OPPE, T. E., PLESS, I. AND APTE, E. (1970), *Children of West Indian Immigrants*, Institute of Race Relations.

HORNBY, P. A. (1977), *Bilingualism — Psychological, Social and Educational Implications*, New York, Academic Press.

HUGHES, M. *et al.* (1980), *Nurseries Now*, Harmondsworth, Penguin.

HUGHILL, B. (1979), 'Wandsworth Parents' Group', *Issues in Race and Education*, No. 21.

HUMPHREY, D. and WARD, M. (1972), *Passports and Politics*, Harmondsworth, Penguin.

HUSBAND, C. (Ed.), (1982), *Race in Britain*, Hutchinson.

INGHAM, E. (1982), 'British and West Indian Children in Day Nurseries. A Comparative Study', *New Community*, Vol. 9, No. 3, Winter/Spring 1982, pp. 423-30.

INNER LONDON EDUCATION AUTHORITY (1967), *The Education of Immigrant Pupils in Primary Schools*, Report of a Working Party of Members of the Inspectorate and Schools Psychological Service (Report No. 959). ILEA.

INNER LONDON EDUCATION AUTHORITY (1979), *Multi-Ethnic Education*, Joint Progress Report of the School Sub-Committee and the Further and Higher Education Sub-Committee, ILEA.

INNER LONDON EDUCATION AUTHORITY (1978), *Grant-Aid to Supplementary School*, Report No. 8689, ILEA.

ISAACS, S. (1946), *Social Development in Young Children. A Study of Beginnings*, Routledge.

JACKSON, K. (1980), 'Some Fallacies in Community Education and their Consequences in Working-Class Areas', in FLETCHER, C. and THOMPSON, N. (Eds.), *Issues in Community Education*, Brighton, Falmer Press.

JACKSON, A. and HANNON, P. (1981), *The Bellfield Reading Project*, Rochdale, Bellfield Community Council.

JACKSON, B. and JACKSON, S. (1979), *Child Minders. A Study in Action-Research*, Routledge.

JEFFERY, P. (1976), *Migrants and Refugees. Muslim and Christian Pakistani Families in Bristol*, Cambridge, CUP.

JOHNSON, D. and RANSOM, E. (1980), 'Parents' Perceptions of Secondary Schools' in CRAFT, M., RAYNOR, J. and COHEN, L. (Eds.), *Linking Home and School* (3rd edition), Harper and Row.

JOHNSON, D. and RANSOM, E. (1983), *Family and School*, Croom Helm.

JONES, D. (1979), 'The Chinese in Britain — Origins and Development of a Community', *New Community*, Vol. 7, No. 3, pp.397-402.

JONES, P. J. (1977), 'An Evaluation of the Effect of Sport on the Integration of West Indian School Children' (Unpublished Ph.D. Thesis), University of Surrey.

KHAN, V. S. (1977), 'The Pakistanis. Mirpuri Villagers at Home and in the City of Bradford' in WATSON, J. (Ed.), *Between Two Cultures*, Oxford, Blackwell.

KHAN, V. S. (Ed.), (1979), *Minority Families in Britain – Support and Stress*, Tavistock.

KHAN, V. S. (1980), *Co-operation Between Schools, Parents and Communities* (Mimeographed Paper), Linguistics Minorities Project, University of London.

KIRKLEES (1981), *Report of the Inter-Directorate Working Party on Multi-Ethnic Kirklees*, Huddersfield.

KIRP, D. L. (1983), *Just Schools. The Ideal of Racial Equality in American Education*, Berkeley, California, University of California Press.

LATHAM, J. (1982), 'Exceptional Children or Exceptional Teachers: An Alternative Policy for Teacher Education in a Multicultural Society', *Journal of Further and Higher Education*, Vol. 6, No. 2.

LAWRENCE, D. (1974), *Black Migrants, White Natives*, CUP.

LEWIS, E. G. (1970), 'Immigrants – Their Language and Development', *Trends in Education*, Vol. 19, Department of Education and Science.

LISTER, D. (1980), 'Black Teachers Face Race Bias in Jobs and Promotion', *Times Educational Supplement*, 3.10.81.

LITTLE, A. and WILLEY, R. (1981), *Multi-Ethnic Education – the Way Forward*, Schools Council Working Paper No. 18.

LOCAL GOVERNMENT ACT (1966), HMSO.

LODGE, B. (1982), 'Libyans Ask for Cash Aid', *Times Educational Supplement*, 29.10.82.

LODGE, B. (1983), 'Putting Their Money Where Their Faith Is', *Times Educational Supplement*, 25.2.83.

LYNCH, J. and PIMLOTT, J. A. (1975), *Parents and Teachers*, Schools Council Research Studies, Macmillan.

LYNCH, J. (Ed.), (1981), *Teaching in the Multicultural School*, Ward Lock Educational.

MABEY, (1981), 'Black British Literacy', *Educational Research*, Vol. 23, No. 2, pp.83-95.

MACBETH, A. (1983), *The Child Between. A Report on School-Family Relations in the Countries of the European Community*, Department of Education, University of Glasgow.

MACMILLAN, K. (1980), 'The Education Welfare Officer – Past, Present and Future' in CRAFT, M., RAYNOR, J. and COHEN, L. (Eds.), *Linking Home and School* (3rd edition), Harper and Row.

MAKINS, V. (1982), 'Asian Preferences to be Met', *Times Educational Supplement*, 11.10.82.

MALIK, S. K. (1982), *A Response to the Report of the Kirklees Interdirectorate Working Party on Multi-Ethnic Kirklees*, Dewsbury, West Yorkshire.

MARETT, V. P. (1976), 'Immigrants in Further Education' (Unpublished M.Ed. Dissertation), University of Leicester.

MARLAND, M. (1974), *Pastoral Care*, Heinemann.

MARSH and SCRIBBENS (1982), 'Educational Home Visiting in Inner London – An Adult Education Model' in APLIN, G. and PUGH, G. (Eds.), *Perspectives on Pre-School Home Visiting*, National Childrens Bureau and Community Education Development Centre.

MCGEENEY, P. (1969), *Parents are Welcome*, Longman.

MCNEAL, J. and ROGERS, M. (1971), *The Multi-Racial School*, Penguin.

MIDWINTER, E. (1972), *Priority – Education*, Harmondsworth, Penguin.

MILNER, D. (1982), 'The Education of the Black Child in Britain. A Review and a Response', *New Community*, Vol. 9, No. 2, pp.289-93.

MILNER, D. (1983), *Children and Race – Ten Years On*, Ward Lock Educational.

MORRISH, I. (1971), *The Background of Immigrant Children*, Allen and Unwin.

MYRDAL, G. (1964), *Challenge to Affluence*, Gollancz.

MUKHERJEE, T. (1982), 'Sri Guru Sabha – Southall' in OHRI, A., MANNING, B. and CURNO, P. (Eds.), *Community Work and Racism*, Routledge.

MUKHERJEE, T. (1983), 'Collusion, Conflict or Constructive Anti-Racist Socialisation' in *Multi-Cultural Teaching*, Vol. 1, No. 2, pp.24-5.

Multiracial Education, Journal of the National Association for Multiracial Education, (formerly *Multiracial School*), Goodwin Press.

MUNGO, C. J. (1979), 'The Use of Dialect of West Indian Origin in British Schools', *Educational Journal*, Vol. 2, No. 1, Commission for Racial Equality.

MUSGROVE, F. (1966), *The Family, Education and Society*, Routledge.

NAIPAUL, V. S. (1982), *Islamic Journey*, Harmondsworth, Penguin.

NATIONAL ASSOCIATION FOR MULTIRACIAL EDUCATION (1983), *Pre-Schooling and Ethnic Minority Children*, Derby, NAME.

NATIONAL COMMITTEE OF PARENT-TEACHER ASSOCIATIONS (1982), *Why a National Confederation?*, 43 Stonebridge Road, Northfleet, Gravesend, Kent.

NATIONAL CHILD-CARE CAMPAIGN and NATIONAL ASSOCIATION OF ONE-PARENT FAMILIES (1983), *Statistics on Cuts*, NCCC.

NATIONAL NURSERY EXAMINATION BOARD (1983), Syllabus, NNEB.

NATIONAL UNION OF TEACHERS (1967), *The NUT View on the Education of Immigrants*, NUT.

NATIONAL UNION OF TEACHERS (1978), *All Our Children*, NUT.

NATIONAL UNION OF TEACHERS (1982a), *Combatting Racialism in School*, NUT.

NATIONAL UNION OF TEACHERS (1982b), *Mother Tongue Teaching*, NUT.

NEIL, A. (1982), 'In Loco Parentis', *Issues in Race and Education*, No. 37, p.6.

New Equals (1982), Newsletter of the Commission for Racial Equality, Autumn.

Newsletter (1983), Black Working Party, National Child-Care Campaign, April/May.

NOOR, S. N. and KHALSA, S. S. (1978), *Educational Needs of Asian Children in the Context of Multiracial Education in Wolverhampton. A Survey of Parents' Views and Attitudes*, Indian Workers' Association, Wolverhampton.

NORBURN, V. and WIGHT, J. (1980), 'Parents, Children and Prejudice', *New Community*, Vol. 8, No. 3.

NORBURN, V. and WIGHT, J. (1982), 'Policies on Racism – What Parents Think', *Where*, No. 182, pp.20-25.

NY KWEE CHOO (1968), *The Chinese in London*, Oxford, OUP.

OAKLEY, R. (1968), *New Backgrounds*, OUP for IRR.

O'CONNOR, M.(1983), 'A Morrell Dilemma', *The Guardian*, 3.5.83.

OFFICE OF POPULATION, CENSUS AND SURVEYS (1971), *Census of Population*, OPCS.

OFFICE OF POPULATION, CENSUS AND SURVEYS (1981), *Census of Population*, OPCS.

ORGANISATION OF AFRICAN AND ASIAN WOMEN (1979), 'Black Education', *Fowadd*.

PARKER, S. (1982), 'Scope for Improvement', *Times Educational Supplement*, 3.12.82.

PATTERSON, S. (1963), *Dark Strangers*, Tavistock.

PEACH, C. (1968), *West Indian Migration to Britain. A Social Geography*, OUP for IRR.

PEACH, C., VAUGHAN, R. and SMITH, S. (Eds.), (1981), *Ethnic Segregation in Cities*, Croom Helm.

PEARSON, D.G. (1981), *Race, Class and Political Activism. A Study of West Indians in Britain*, Farnborough, Gower Press.

PHIZAKLEA, A. (1982), 'Migrant Women and Wage Labour. The Case of West Indian Women in Britain', in WEST, J. (Ed.), *Work, Women and the Labour Market*, Routledge.

PLOWDEN REPORT (1967), *Children and Their Primary Schools*, HMSO.

PRYCE, K. (1979), *Endless Pressure. A Study of West Indians in Bristol*, Harmondsworth, Penguin.

RAMPTON CONFERENCE REPORT (1981), (opened by Sir Keith Joseph to debate the Rampton Report), *West Indian Children in Our Schools*, DES.

RATCLIFFE, P. (1981), *Racism and Reaction*, Routledge.

RAVEN, J. (1980), *Parents, Teachers and Children. A Study of Educational Home-Visiting Schemes*, Hodder and Stoughton for SCRE.

RAY, RADHIKA R. (1982), 'Colour Code', Letter to *Times Educational Supplement*, 8.1.82.

REDBRIDGE STUDY, (1978), *Cause for Concern, West Indian Pupils in Redbridge*, Redbridge and Black Parents' Progressive Association, Community Relations Council.

REEVES, F. and CHEVANNES, M. (1981), 'The Underachievement of Rampton', *Multiracial Education*, Vol. 10, No. 1, pp.35-42.

REX, J. (1971), *Race Relations in Sociological Theory*, Weidenfeld and Nicolson.

REX, J. (1981), 'Equality of Opportunity and the Minority Child in British Schools', Paper Presented to Conference on the Rampton Report, University of London Institute of Education, Nov. 1981.

REX, J. and MOORE, (1967), *Race, Community and Conflict*, OUP for IRR.

REX, J. and TOMLINSON, S. (1979), *Colonial Immigrants in a British City – A Class Analysis*, Routledge.

RICHARDS, K. J. (1983), 'A Contribution to the Multicultural Education Debate', *New Community*, Vol. 10, No. 2, pp. 222-5.

RIST, R. (1970), 'Student Social Class and Teacher Expectations. The Self-Fulfilling Prophecy in Ghetto Education', *Harvard Educational Review*, Vol. 40, No. 3.

ROBERTS, K. (1980), 'Schools, Parents and Social Class' in CRAFT, M., RAYNOR, J. and COHEN, L. (Eds.), *Linking Home and School*, Harper and Row.

ROSE, E. J. B. and Associates (1969), *Colour and Citizenship. A Report on Race Relations in Britain*, OUP for IRR.

ROSENTHAL, R. and JACOBSON, L. (1968), *Pygmalion in the Classroom*, Holt, Rinehart and Winston, New York.

RUBOVITS, P. C. and MAEHR, M. (1973), 'Pygmalion Black and White', *Journal of Personality and Social Psychology*, Vol. 25, No. 2.

RUTTER, M. *et al.* (1974), 'Children of West Indian Immigrants, 1. Rates of Behavioural Deviance and Psychiatric Disorder', *Journal of Child Psychology and Psychiatry*, Vol. 15, pp.241-62.

SCHOOL REPORTS (1979), *Newsletter*, No. 1, Slough, NFER.

SECONDARY HEADS ASSOCIATION (1982), *Review,* Vol. LXXVII, No. 240. pp.486-8, SHA.

SELECT COMMITTEE ON RACE RELATIONS AND IMMIGRATION (1973), *Education*, HMSO.

SHARROCK, A. (1980), 'Research on Home-School Relations', in CRAFT, M., RAYNOR, J. and COHEN, L. (Eds.), *Linking Home and School* (3rd edition), Harper and Row.

SIMOES, A. (1976), *The Bilingual Child, Research and Analysis of Existing Themes*, New York, Academic Press.

SMITH, D. (1977), *Racial Disadvantage in Britain*, Penguin.

SPENCER, D. (1981), 'More Action Needed in Politics – Black Staff Told', *Times Educational Supplement*, 18.12.81.

SPENCER, D. (1982a), 'Asians Look to Mainstream as only Long-Term Answer', *Times Educational Supplement*, 12.3.82.

SPENCER, D. (1982b), 'Brent to Investigate Race Bias Complaint', *Times Educational Supplement*, 15.10.82.

SPENCER, D. (1983), 'Authority Seeks Blacks' Views on Ethnic Policy', *Times Educational Supplement*, 18.3.83.

STONE, M. (1981), *The Education of the Black Child in Britain*, Fontana.

SUMMERFIELD, P. (1982), *Women Workers in the Second World War* (Unpublished D.Phil. Thesis), University of Sussex.

Sunday Times (1983), Interview with the Rt. Hon. Mrs M. Thatcher, Prime Minister, 27.2.83.

SUTCLIFFE, D. (1978), 'The Language of First and Second Generation West Indian Children in Bedfordshire' (Unpublished M.Ed. Thesis), University of Leicester.

SUTCLIFFE, D.(1982), *Black British English*, Oxford, Blackwell.

TANNA, K. (1981), 'Gujerati Muslim Parents in Lancaster – Their Views on Education' (Unpublished Independent Study for B.A. Degree), University of Lancaster.

TAYLOR, M. J. (1981), *Caught Between – A Review of Research into the Education of Pupils of West Indian Origin*, Slough, NFER.

TAYLOR REPORT (DES) (1977), *A New Partnership for our Schools*, HMSO.

Times Educational Supplement (1982), 'ILEA Relents on New Bengali School', 23.7.82.

Times Educational Supplement, (1983), 'Ceremonial dagger poses problems' 11.2.83.

TINKER, H. (1979), 'A Passage to Limbo', *Higher Education*, Vol. 8, pp.573-83.

TIZARD, B., MORTIMORE, J. and BURCHELL, B. (1981), *Involving Parents in Nursery and Infant Schools. A Source-Book for Teachers*, Grant McIntyre.

TIZARD, J., MOSS, P. and PERRY, J. (1976), *All Our Children – Pre-School Services in a Changing Society*, Temple Smith.

TOMLINSON, S. (1980), 'Ethnic Minority Parents and Education' in CRAFT, M., RAYNOR, J. and COHEN, L. (Eds.), *Linking Home and School* (3rd edition), Harper and Row.

TOMLINSON, S. (1981), 'Multiracial Schooling – Parents and Teachers' Views', *Education 3-13*, Vol. 9, No. 1.

TOMLINSON, S. (1982), *A Sociology of Special Education*, Routledge.

TOMLINSON, S. (1983), 'The Educational Performance of Children of Asian Origin', *New Community*, Vol. 10, No. 3, pp.381-92.

TOWNSEND, H. E. R. and BRITTAN, E. (1972), *Organisation in Multiracial Schools*, NFER.

TWITCHEN, J. and DEMUTH, C. (1981), *Multicultural Education*, BBC Publications.

UNION OF MUSLIM ORGANISATIONS OF UNITED KINGDOM AND EIRE (1975), *Islamic Education and Single-Sex Schools*, UMO.

UNION OF MUSLIM ORGANISATIONS OF UNITED KINGDOM AND EIRE (1978), *National Muslim Education Council – Background Papers*, UMO.

VAN DER EYKEN, W. (1982), *Home-Start – A Four-Year Evaluation*, Leicester, Home-Start Consultancy.

VELLIMS, S. (1982), 'South Asian Students in British Universities – A Statistical Note', *New Community*, Vol. 10, No. 2, pp. 206-12.

VENNING, P. (1983), 'Menacing Warning Sent to Haringey Heads over Exams', *Times Educational Supplement*, 11.2.83.

WALKER, M. (1977), *The National Front*, Routledge.

WALLER, W. (1932), *The Sociology of Teaching*, New York, Wiley.

WANG, B. (1982), 'Chinese Children in Britain', unpublished paper from Conference on Multi-Ethnic Education, College of St Peter and St Paul, Cheltenham.

WATSON, J. L. (Ed.), (1977), *Between Two Cultures*, Oxford, Blackwell.

WELLUM, J. (1981), *Survey of Library Needs of Black Supplementary Schools*, North London Polytechnic.

West Indian World (1977), 'Call For Black Schools', 6.10.77.

WILCE, H. (1983), 'Co-operation Pledge Plan Drawn up for Parents', *Times Educational Supplement*, 25.3.83.

WOODFORD, ORVILLE, (1982), Interview on 'Ebony', BBC TV, 17.11.82.

WORLD COUNCIL OF CHURCHES (1982), *Christians and Education in a Multi-Faith World*, WCC.

WORRALL, M. (1978), 'Multiracial Britain and the Third World – Tensions and Approaches in the Classroom', *New Approaches in Multiracial Education*, Vol. 6, No. 3.

WORRELL, K.(1972), 'All-Black Schools – An Answer to Under-Performance', *Race Today*, January.

YATES, O. (1982), *Final Report of the Van Leer/Open University Project on Parenting Materials* (Unpublished Report for Birmingham LEA), Birmingham.

Index